REFERENCE GUIDES IN LITERATURE
NUMBER 4
Joseph Katz, *General Editor*

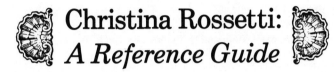

# Christina Rossetti:
## *A Reference Guide*

R. W. Crump

G. K. HALL & CO., 70 LINCOLN STREET, BOSTON, MASS.

Library of Congress Cataloging in Publication Data

Crump, Rebecca W    1944-
   Christina Rossetti : a reference guide.

   Includes index.
   1.  Rossetti, Christina Georgina, 1830-1894--Bibli-
ography.
Z8759.75.C76  [PR5238]    016.821'8       75-28008
ISBN 0-8161-7847-X

**Other books in the Reference Guide Series:**

*Sylvia Plath and Anne Sexton: A Reference Guide* • Cameron
   Northouse and Thomas P. Walsh, No. 1

*John Osborne: A Reference Guide* • Cameron Northouse and
   Thomas P. Walsh, No. 2

*Frank Norris: A Reference Guide* • Jesse S. Crisler and
   Joseph R. McElrath, Jr., No. 3

*Edith Wharton and Kate Chopin: A Reference Guide* •
   Marlene Springer, No. 5

*Washington Irving: A Reference Guide* • Haskell
   Springer, No. 6

*This publication is printed on permanent/durable acid-free paper.*
MANUFACTURED IN THE UNITED STATES OF AMERICA

# Contents

Introduction. . . . . . . . . . . . . . . . . . . . . . vii

Writings About Christina Rossetti (1862–1973) . . . .   1

Index . . . . . . . . . . . . . . . . . . . . . . . 143

# Introduction

Christina Rossetti (1830-1894) was born into a family distinguished by its considerable literary talents and interests. Her grandfather, Gaetano Polidori, owned his own printing press and produced a book of Christina's verses in 1847 (her earliest printed volume). Christina's father, Gabriele Rossetti, and her older sister, Maria Francesca Rossetti, were scholars of Dante Alighieri; her oldest brother, Dante Gabriel Rossetti, was the famous Pre-Raphaelite poet and painter; and her brother William Michael Rossetti is best known as the editor of the poems, prose writings, and correspondence of both Christina and Dante Gabriel Rossetti.

In the literary atmosphere of this gifted family, Christina was encouraged to pursue her own poetic genius and to publish her works of fiction and verse. Her first published volume of poetry, Goblin Market and Other Poems, received considerable attention, mostly favorable, when it appeared in 1862; her successive volumes, issued over the next thirty-two years, helped to secure her reputation as one of the foremost English poetesses of the nineteenth century. In the reviews and articles written about her during her lifetime, she was compared with Elizabeth Barrett Browning for the beauty of her sonnets; with Samuel Taylor Coleridge for her originality of imagery and meter; with William Blake, Jean Ingelow, and Emily Brontë for her clear diction and lyrical simplicity; with such Pre-Raphaelite poets as Dante Gabriel Rossetti for the combination of mysticism and materialism in her poetry; and with Herbert, Vaughan, and Crashaw for the fervor and spiritual penetration of her devotional verse.

# INTRODUCTION

Four years after her death, her close friend and admirer, Mackenzie Bell, published what remains the most exhaustive biography to date (See 1898.A1). All of the subsequent biographies depend to a greater or lesser extent on Bell's work. William Michael Rossetti's famous "Memoir" (1904.B10), prefacing an edition of her poems which he produced in 1904, has proved to be another valuable source of information for later biographers. His edition itself remains the most complete collection of her poetry, although it lacks over one hundred of Christina's poems.

After 1904 the interest in Christina and her work suffered a decline. For the next twenty-five years, almost all of the writings about her took the form of short articles, sketches, and reminiscences, although there were a few masters theses and one dissertation. For the most part, these writings are biographical rather than critical in nature. The biographical interest continued to predominate in the centennial books of the 1930's as well as in most of the studies written during the next thirty years. Scholars theorized about the extent to which Christina's poems were autobiographical and debated which particular events she had in mind when writing specific poems. Many believed that her refusal to marry her first suitor, James Collinson, haunted her for the rest of her life (See 1931.A1, 1932.B1, 1932.B8, 1933.B4, 1949.A1, 1955.A1). Others believed that many of her poems were written about her second suitor, Charles Cayley, whom she also rejected (See 1919.B3, 1929.B3, 1930.A1, 1931.A2, 1970.B2). The most controversial biography was written in 1963 by Lona Mosk Packer (1963.A1). Packer argues that Christina was in love with William Bell Scott, a close friend of Dante Gabriel Rossetti, and that Scott was the subject of much of Christina's enigmatic love poetry.

While scholars labored to solve the biographical mysteries surrounding Christina's literary productions, critical questions concerning Christina's poetic techniques and literary merits continued to be largely neglected, with some notable exceptions. Anna Ruth Bourne

# Introduction

(1920.A1), Edith Birkhead (1930.A1), and June Inez Lingo (1930.A2) place Christina's work in the context of the Pre-Raphaelite Movement; Justine Frederika de Wilde (1923.A2) compares Christina's poetic craftsmanship with that of her brother Dante Gabriel Rossetti; Marjorie A. Bald (1923.B1) and B. Ifor Evans (1933.B2) consider some of the literary influences reflected in Christina's poetry; and there have been a number of works comparing Christina with Elizabeth Barrett Browning (1927.A1, 1939.A1) and with Emily Dickinson (1931.A4, 1933.A1). In the last ten years, however, a shift in emphasis has occurred, and Christina has finally begun to receive more consideration as a serious literary artist and craftsman; for example, Winston Weathers discusses three of the major motifs in her poems--the "divided self," the "broken betrothal," and the "voices of the dead" (See 1965.B3). A. A. DeVitas analyzes the use of allegory in "Goblin Market" in a brief note (1968.B4); and in "A Note on the Imagery in Christina Rossetti's 'A Birthday,'" Richard D. Lynde examines the numerous associations with the world of trade in Victorian England, the paintings of Dante Gabriel Rossetti, and the Bible, which are reflected in that poem (See 1965.B2).

Concomitant with these articles are several book-length studies, namely Thomas Burnett Swann's Wonder and Whimsey:  The Fantastic World of Christina Rossetti (1960.A1) and Gisela Hönnighausen's Christina Rossetti als Viktorianische Dichterin (1969.A2); both treat, among other topics, the emblematic techniques in Christina's poetry.  Furthermore, the number of dissertations offering critical assessments of Christina's work has increased in the last decade (See 1967.B1, 1969.A1, 1969.A4, and 1971.A1).  But these critical studies and articles serve primarily as a tantalizing suggestion of what remains to be done--a comprehensive examination and evaluation of Christina's literary accomplishments.

The present annotated secondary bibliography includes reminiscences, memorials, sketches, essays, parodies, articles, theses, dissertations, book-length studies, chapters of books, reviews of Christina's works,

# Introduction

introductions from selective editions of Christina's poetry, introductions from the major anthologies of Victorian poetry which include Christina, and reviews of
works about Christina which include comments on her.
Works or reviews which merely mention Christina in passing, adding little or nothing to a knowledge of her life
or work, are omitted. Examples of such an omission are
Anne Kimball Tuell's Mrs. Meynell and Her Literary Generation (New York: Dutton, 1925) and Percy F. Bick-
nell's review of Ford Madox Hueffer's Ancient Lights
(London: Chapman and Hall, 1911), in Dial, L (1911),
345-46.

The following abbreviations are used in the
bibliography:

| | |
|---|---|
| AntigR | Antigonish Review |
| BNYPL | Bulletin of the New York Public Library |
| HAB | Humanities Association Bulletin (Canada) |
| JPC | Journal of Popular Culture (Bowling Green University) |
| N&Q | Notes and Queries |
| PMLA | Publications of the Modern Language Association of America |
| PULC | Princeton University Library Chronicle |
| RES | Review of English Studies |
| SatR | Saturday Review |
| SCN | Seventeenth-Century News |
| TLS | Times Literary Supplement [London] |
| UTQ | University of Toronto Quarterly |
| VN | Victorian Newsletter |
| VP | Victorian Poetry (West Virginia University) |
| WHR | Western Humanities Review |
| YR | Yale Review |

The index lists the names of all of the authors of
works about Christina in the bibliography as well as the
titles of all of the books included in the bibliography.
The entries are also indexed by subject, such as "bibliography," "biography (book-length)," and "critical
studies (book-length)." Shorter writings which appear
as chapters or sections of books are indexed by author

# INTRODUCTION

and by the name of the book rather than the title of the chapter. Christina's reviews are indexed under the title of the work they review. Short articles and notes with such general or popular titles as "Christina Rossetti" or "Christina Rossetti's Poems" (there are over eighty such cases) are indexed by author and subject rather than by title.

For guidance in preparing this bibliography I am particularly indebted to Professor Oscar Maurer of the University of Texas. My work has also benefited from the detailed corrections and suggestions made by Professors Maurine McElroy, Gordon Mills, and Robert Wilson, of the University of Texas. I would like to express my special appreciation to Kathleen Blow, Head Reference Librarian at the University of Texas, as well as to the members of Interlibrary Borrowing--Kathleen Gaddy, JoAnne Hawkins, and Sheila Winship--for their efficiency in locating and obtaining books and articles which were not in the University of Texas libraries.

WRITINGS ABOUT CHRISTINA ROSSETTI

1862 A  BOOKS - NONE

1862 B  SHORTER WRITINGS

1    ANON. "Miss Rossetti's Goblin Market," Eclectic
     Review, NS II (June), 493-99.
         The reviewer finds traces of the influence
     of Herbert and Tennyson in the volume, but
     praises it for its originality, as well as
     its freshness, which he finds in such poems
     as "From House to Home":  "The volume has
     very decided character and originality, both
     in theme and treatment; it is also a volume
     upon which many readers would pronounce a
     very hasty verdict--of rubbish, perhaps, un-
     less themselves gifted in some measure with
     that faculty of insight into the occult and
     dark which is not always possessed even by
     true poets."

2    ANON. "Miss Rossetti's Goblin Market," Living
     Age, LXXIV (26 July), 147-50.
     Reprint of 1862.B1.

3    ANON. "Poems by Mr. and Miss Rossetti," Ecclesi-
     astic and Theologian, XXIV (September), 419-
     29.
         Only pp. 427-29 are devoted to a discussion
     of Goblin Market and Other Poems; the rest of
     the review concerns Dante Gabriel Rossetti's
     The Early Italian Poets, which came out in

(ANON.)
1861. "Goblin Market" is found to be care-
lessly composed and far inferior to such
pieces as "Up-Hill" and "Advent," which are
quoted here. The reviewer notes the "two
rather grotesque wood-cuts exceedingly Prae-
Raphaelesque [sic] in character" and in conclusion asks Christina Rossetti to "give to
the reading public something better than anything in the book before us."

4    ANON. Review of Goblin Market and Other Poems,
     Athenaeum, No. 1800 (26 April), 557-58.
        The contents of Goblin Market and Other
     Poems are summarized, and the volume is
     praised for its naturalness and freshness.
     "Goblin Market" has "true dramatic charac-
     ter." "An Apple Gathering" is quoted. The
     reviewer notes an unevenness in some of the
     poetry, due to an overabundance of sorrow and
     harsh verbal discord.

5    ANON. Review of Goblin Market and Other Poems,
     British Quarterly Review, XXXVI (July), 230-
     31.
        The volume is praised for its beauty, ten-
     derness, and art. The reviewer likes the de-
     votional pieces best, although "Goblin Mar-
     ket" is the poem which is "most purely and
     completely a work of art."

6    ANON. Review of Goblin Market and Other Poems,
     SatR, XIII (24 May), 595-96.
        The reviewer approves most of the poems ex-
     cept "Goblin Market," which is "a story of
     too flimsy and unsubstantial character to
     justify or to bear the elaborate detail with
     which it is worked out." He praises "Up-
     Hill" as one of the best poems of the volume

(ANON.)
and notes the graceful style of "An Apple
Gathering." He concludes with the hope that
Christina Rossetti will learn that "quaintness is not strength, and that it generally
interferes with beauty."


1863 A   BOOKS - NONE

1863 B   SHORTER WRITINGS

1      NORTON, MRS. CHARLES ELIOT. "'The Angel in the
       House,' and 'The Goblin Market,'" Macmillan's
       Magazine, VIII (September), 398-404.
            Norton considers "Goblin Market" to be "in-
       comparably the best of her compositions." It
       vies with Coleridge's "Rime of the Ancient
       Mariner" in its "vivid and wonderful power by
       which things unreal and mystic are made to
       blend and link themselves with the everyday
       images and events of common life." There are
       extensive quotations from "Goblin Market."

2      _____. "'The Angel in the House,' and 'The Gob-
       lin Market,'" Living Age, LXXIX (17 October),
       124-29.
       Reprint of 1863.B1.


1864 A   BOOKS - NONE

1864 B   SHORTER WRITINGS

1.     ANON. [A Campaigner at Home.] "Our Camp in the
       Woodland: A Day with the Gentle Poets,"
       Fraser's, LXX (August), 204-13.
            The article is a discussion of the poetry of
       Elizabeth Barrett Browning, Adelaide Procter,

1864

(ANON.)
Jean Ingelow, and Christina Rossetti. The
article quotes some of Christina Rossetti's
poems, such as "Three Seasons," "An Apple
Gathering," "Rest," and "Dreamland," and describes Christina Rossetti's work as "bold,
vigorous, peculiar, daring." She is "the
slave neither of forms nor of ideas."

1865 A    BOOKS - NONE

1865 B    SHORTER WRITINGS

1    DALLAS, ENEAS SWEETLAND. "Modern Poets," [Lon-
     don] Times (11 January), 12, col. 5.
         This paragraph gives a comparison of Jean
     Ingelow and Christina Rossetti. Christina
     Rossetti's poetical art is "simpler, firmer
     and deeper" than Jean Ingelow's, although
     Christina Rossetti is not so ambitious in her
     choice of subject as is Jean Ingelow.

1866 A    BOOKS - NONE

1866 B    SHORTER WRITINGS

1    ANON. "Miss Rossetti's New Poems," Spectator,
     XXXIX (1 September), 974-75.
         A review of The Prince's Progress and Other
     Poems. The reviewer feels this volume to be
     inferior to Goblin Market: "With few excep-
     tions the fugitive insights and glimpses of
     beauty with which these poems abound have
     little to bind them together, and leave
     little mark on the mind." He quotes part of
     "A Bird's Eye View" as an example of silly,
     fanciful verse, and quotes all of "Light Love"

(ANON.)

as the finest poem in the volume. He concludes: "The imagination which conceived
Goblin Market and the very different kind of
poem we have just extracted ought to be ca-
pable of other original efforts, and we think
would be, if Miss Rossetti would only concen-
trate her powers more, and instead of throw-
ing off so many slight snatches of mere
prettiness, would cherish one or two subjects
long in her imagination, and not attempt to
write upon them until they had really taken
root,--taken possession of her mind."

2    ANON. "Miss Rossetti's Poems," Eclectic Review,
CXXIV (August), 124-30.
A review of The Prince's Progress and Other
Poems. The reviewer praises this volume for
having the same "excellence of beauty" as
Goblin Market, and quotes "Weary in Well-
Doing," "Gone for Ever," "Life and Death,"
"Despised and Rejected," "Good Friday," and
"Bird or Beast," among others.

3    ANON. "Miss Rossetti's Poems," The Nation, III
(19 July), 47-48.
A review of The Prince's Progress and Other
Poems. The reviewer notes that "it being natural to her to give form and color to her
idea, to give it a body, to be dissatisfied
if it is not made definite and perfectly
clear, it is natural for her as an artist, in
order that the reader may see and feel as she
sees and feels, to draw in very sharp outline
and to color with all the vividness possible."
He quotes from such poems as "Song" ("Two
doves upon the self-same branch") and "A
Year's Windfalls" to illustrate his point.

1866

4    ANON.  "Miss Rossetti's Poems," Reader, VII
          (30 June), 613.
             A review of The Prince's Progress and Other
          Poems.  The reviewer finds "Life and Death"
          to be the best poem rather than "The Prince's
          Progress," which is too long to suit Christina
          Rossetti's genius for short lyrical thoughts.
          The volume as a whole is considered to be "the
          pleasantest volume of verse which this year
          has given us."

5    ANON.  "Miss Rossetti's Poems," Living Age, XC
          (18 August), 441-42.
          Reprint of 1866.B4.

6    ANON.  "Miss Rossetti's Poems," SatR, XXI
          (23 June), 761-62.
             A review of The Prince's Progress and Other
          Poems.  Christina Rossetti is praised as an
          excellent minor poet.  The reviewer finds a
          lack of subtle suggestion in "The Prince's
          Progress":  the "profusion of figure and color
          and movement, charming as it is, makes us
          alive to the want of a dim and suggestive
          background."

7    ANON.  "Miss Rossetti's Poems," Eclectic Magazine
          of Foreign Literature, NS IV (September),
          322-25.
          Reprint of 1866.B6.

8    ANON.  Review of The Prince's Progress and Other
          Poems, Athenaeum, No. 2017 (23 June), 824-25.
             The reviewer compares "The Prince's Prog-
          ress" and "Goblin Market":  both are allego-
          ries of temptation away from a worthy and
          earnest life, except that whereas temptation
          is overcome in "Goblin Market," temptations
          triumph in "The Prince's Progress."  The

(ANON.)
allegory of "The Prince's Progress" is saved
from stiffness by vivid description; we do
not see a conflict of the heart but the se-
quel to that conflict. The reviewer praises
the volume as a whole and concludes with a
quotation from "Maiden-Song."

9      [DENNETT, J. R.]  "Miss Rossetti's Poems," Nation (New York), III (19 July), 47-48.
A review of The Prince's Progress and Other
Poems.  Dennett describes the poems as "Pre-
Raphaelite" and praises them for their quaintness, pictorial vividness, and life.  He finds
the devotional poems inferior to the other
poems because they seem to be imitative of
George Herbert's work.


1867 A  BOOKS - NONE

1867 B  SHORTER WRITINGS

1      [RUDD, F. A.]  "Christina G. Rossetti," Catholic
World, IV (March), 839-46.
This is a review of Goblin Market and Other
Poems and The Prince's Progress and Other
Poems, which were published together in a
single volume by Roberts Brothers of Boston in
1866.  Rudd finds fault with the excessive
melancholy exhibited in these poems, and
states that "Goblin Market" and "The Prince's
Progress" rival for the distinction of being
the worst poem of the volume.  "For imagination, she offers fantasy; for sentiment, sen-
timentality; for aspiration, ambition; for
originality and thought, little or nothing;
for melody, fantastic janglings of words; and
these, with all tenderness for the ill-starred

1867

([RUDD, F. A.])
intensity of purpose that could fetch them so far·, are no more poetry than the industrious Virginia colonists' shiploads of mica were gold."


1868 A   BOOKS - NONE

1868 B   SHORTER WRITINGS

1    ANON. "Poetesses," SatR, XXV (23 May), 678-79.
        The writer finds Elizabeth Browning, Christina Rossetti, and Emily Brontë the only true poetesses of the century on the basis of the intensity of their verse. Of Christina Rossetti: "We do not think her naturally so strong a genius as Emily Brontë; but her imaginative power is decidedly greater." The beauty of "Goblin Market" appears "unquestionable."

2    ANON. "Poetesses," Living Age, XCVII (27 June), 819-22.
        Reprint of 1868.B1.


1869 A   BOOKS - NONE

1869 B   SHORTER WRITINGS

1    [FORMAN, HARRY BUXTON.] "Criticisms on Contemporaries: No. VI. The Rossettis. Part I," Tinsley's Magazine, V (August), 59-67.
        Christina Rossetti has not yet surpassed Elizabeth Barrett Browning. The Pre-Raphaelite movement was a strong but "baneful" influence on Christina Rossetti for encouraging commonplace "actuality" in some of her poems.

([FORMAN, HARRY BUXTON])
    Forman dislikes the "grotesque" elements of
"Goblin Market" which mar its elegance. "No
Thank You, John" exhibits an actuality result-
ing in flatness. Forman notes that her prose
is inferior to her poetry.

## 1870 A  BOOKS – NONE

## 1870 B  SHORTER WRITINGS

1    ANON. Review of Commonplace and Other Short
Stories, Athenaeum, No. 2223 (4 June), 734–35.
    The reviewer finds "Commonplace" to be the
best of the group: although the plot is conventional, it is told with remarkable finish
and grace. "Vanna's Twins" recalls the manner
of Miss Thackeray. The reviewer concludes
that the volume is, on the whole, a successful
one.

2    ANON. Review of Commonplace and Other Short
Stories, Spectator, XLIII (29 October),
1292–93.
    The reviewer admits Christina Rossetti's
"indisputable claim to be read and noticed"
because of such poems as "Goblin Market," but
with these short stories he finds "the spell
broken." The stories are "wanting in originality and power."

3    SIMCOX, G. A. Review of Commonplace and Other
Short Stories, Academy, I (9 July), 252.
    The real value lies in its "kind quiet cyn-
icism" which is the "only right way to look at
most of our lives."

1871

1871 A   BOOKS - NONE

1871 B   SHORTER WRITINGS

1    ANON. Review of <u>Commonplace and Other Short
     Stories</u>, <u>London Quarterly Review</u>, XXXVI
     (April), 258-29.
         The characters of "Commonplace" are drawn
     with "admirable precision and insight." The
     reviewer compares this short story with the
     novels of Jane Austen. He finds the moral to
     "The Waves of This Troublesome World" to be
     an example of "narrow sectarianism," but ad-
     mires the book on the whole.

2    [FORMAN, HARRY BUXTON.] "VII.  Christina
     Gabriela [sic] Rossetti" in <u>Our Living Poets:
     An Essay in Criticism</u>. London:  Tinsley, pp.
     229-53.
         The first part of the essay is a reprint of
     1869.B1, followed by a review of <u>Commonplace
     and Other Short Stories</u>. Forman finds the
     volume to be charming, thoughtful, and at
     times highly artistic, but not of the same
     strength and vitality as <u>Mansfield Park</u> or
     <u>Northanger Abbey</u>.  "The Lost Titian" is "a
     brilliant sketch of artistic life in Venice."
     Forman finds in this volume of tales a certain
     "half-grotesque simplicity of incident treated
     with a naïveté that makes the reader ready to
     laugh at first and ends by moving him
     profoundly."

1872 A   BOOKS - NONE

1872 B   SHORTER WRITINGS

1    ANON. Review of <u>Sing-Song</u>, <u>Athenaeum</u>, No. 2306
     (6 January), 11.

(ANON.)
Christina Rossetti is praised for writing "some of the saddest as well as the sweetest verses of our time," and Hughes's woodcuts are also praised.

2    ANON. Review of Sing-Song, Harper's Magazine, XLIV (January), 299.
The reviewer notes approvingly the appearance of this volume "rich in song and picture."

3    ANON. Review of Sing-Song, Scribner's Monthly, III (March), 629.
"There are a few poems amongst these sing-songs which Miss Rossetti might have put with her profoundly serious work, and many which will haunt pensive children of maturer years than those whom they were nominally written for."

4    COLVIN, SIDNEY. Review of Sing-Song, Academy, III (15 January), 23-24.
The book is described as "one of the most exquisite of its class ever seen."

1874 A   BOOKS - NONE

1874 B   SHORTER WRITINGS

1    ANON. Review of Speaking Likenesses, Academy, VI (5 December), 606.
"This will probably be one of the most popular children's books this winter. We wish we could understand it."

2    ANON. Review of Speaking Likenesses, Athenaeum, No. 2461 (26 December), 878.

1874

(ANON.)
The reviewer notes that the book "would
have been more original if Alice had never
been to 'Wonderland.'"

1876 A   BOOKS - NONE

1876 B   SHORTER WRITINGS

1     ANON.  "Christina Rossetti's Poems," <u>Catholic</u>
      <u>World</u>, XXIV (October), 122-29.
          This is a review of <u>Goblin Market</u>, <u>The</u>
      <u>Prince's Progress and Other Poems</u>.  The re-
      viewer considers Christina Rossetti to be the
      "queen of the Preraphaelite school," and
      gives a description of the goals and major
      works of that group.  He then demonstrates
      how such poems as "Goblin Market," "The Poor
      Ghost," and "The Prince's Progress" are Pre-
      Raphaelite in nature.  Except for the devo-
      tional poems, Christina Rossetti's poems are
      "not nearly so great as her brother's; indeed,
      they will not stand comparison with them at
      all.  The style is too varied, the pieces are
      too short and fugitive to be stamped with any
      marked originality or individuality, with the
      exception, perhaps, of the 'Goblin Market.'"
      But in her devotional poems Christina Rossetti
      reigns supreme, singing "in strains sad,
      sweet, tender, and musical that a saint might
      envy."

2     ANON.  Review of <u>Goblin Market</u>, <u>The Prince's</u>
      <u>Progress and Other Poems</u>, <u>Literary World</u>
      (Boston), VI (May), 181-82.
          Although Christina Rossetti cannot be reck-
      oned among the popular poets, this volume is
      characterized by sweetness and simplicity,

12

(ANON.)
    tenderness and pathos. "One needs a peculiar
mental temperament in order fully to appre-
ciate her poems."


1877 A  BOOKS - NONE

1877 B  SHORTER WRITINGS

1    [TAYLOR, BAYARD.] Review of Goblin Market, The
    Prince's Progress and Other Poems, Interna-
    tional Review, IV (February), 109-10.
       Christina Rossetti is judged to be inferior
    to Jean Ingelow in "brilliancy of rhetoric,
    rhythmical movement and a certain intensity
    and vividness of apprehension," although
    Christina Rossetti is "simpler, more natural
    and unstudied" than Jean Ingelow. Poetry
    such as "Sleep at Sea" or "Twilight Calm" may
    serve as an echo to "fancies or cravings
    equally vague and unformed: but it can never
    permanently belong to literature."


1879 A  BOOKS - NONE

1879 B  SHORTER WRITINGS

1    COOPER, THOMPSON. "Rossetti, Christina Georgina"
    in Men of the Time: A Dictionary of Contem-
    poraries, Containing Biographical Notices of
    Eminent Characters of Both Sexes, Tenth edi-
    tion. London: Routledge, p. 856.
       Cooper lists some of Christina Rossetti's
    best known volumes of poetry and prose.


1880 A  BOOKS - NONE

1880

1880 B  SHORTER WRITINGS

 1    TAYLOR, BAYARD. "Christina Rossetti" in Crit-
      ical Essays and Literary Notes. New York:
      G. P. Putnam's Sons, pp. 330-32.
      Reprint of 1877.B1.

1881 A  BOOKS - NONE

1881 B  SHORTER WRITINGS

 1    ANON. "Literature," Athenaeum, No. 2811 (10 Sep-
      tember), 327-28.
         A review of A Pageant and Other Poems. The
      reviewer notes Christina Rossetti's love of
      allegory and symbol, as in the poem personify-
      ing the months of the year. He also finds
      the sonnets "charming."

 2    ANON. "Miss Rossetti's New Poems," Eclectic
      Magazine, NS XXXIV (November), 708-12.
      Reprint of 1881.B1.

 3    ANON. "Miss Rossetti's 'Pageant' and Other
      Poems," Literary World, XII (22 October),
      372-73.
         The sonnets comprise the best poetry of the
      volume, especially "Shame is a Shadow" (Later
      Life, No. 13), which is quoted here. "The
      grave and pensive tone . . . rises toward the

1881

(ANON.)
end into a series of strictly religious poems,
which sound like the outcry of a bruised and
bleeding heart. Miss Rossetti's measures
have often a labored originality, which it re-
quires some care on the part of the reader to
follow; but occasionally she falls into a
strain of the truest melody, and carols
blithely like a bird."

4    ANON. Review of A Pageant and Other Poems,
       British Quarterly Review, LXXIV (October),
       480-81.
           The volume is full of "graceful fanciful-
       ness," but her pessimistic verse shows "far
       too much of the processes of her thinking:
       we see the movement of the despairing intel-
       lect far too clearly through the thin veil of
       imagination and fantasy."

5    ANON. "The Rossettis," Literary World, XII
       (5 November), 395-96.
           A review of A Pageant and Other Poems. "A
       Prodigal Son" and "A Martyr" show an "evident
       growth in feeling and in power." Of the
       "Monna Innominata" sonnets, the reviewer
       states, "Even Mrs. Browning's sonnets, dis-
       guised as translations from the Portuguese,
       are less beautiful in form, less self-forget-
       ful in spirit than these."

6    CAINE, T. HALL. Review of A Pageant and Other
       Poems, Academy, XX (27 August), 152.
           Caine praises Christina Rossetti's "A Pag-
       eant," "Ballad of Boding," "Brandon's Both,"
       and "Golden Silences."

7    SIMCOX, G. A. Review of Called to Be Saints,
       Academy, XX (5 November), 341.

15

(SIMCOX, G. A.)
Simcox notes the unevenness of quality in
the book. The "memorial" is successful; a
section of the "Ox" echoes Walt Whitman. "In
general, the writer's natural history is not
very delightful." He praises the hymns for
St. John the Evangelist, the Holy Innocents,
and St. John the Baptist's Day.


1882 A   BOOKS - NONE

1882 B   SHORTER WRITINGS

1    ANON. "New Poetry of the Rossettis and Others,"
     Atlantic Monthly, XLIX (January), 121
        The "Later Life" sonnets are considered the
     best part of the book; the "Monna Innominata"
     sonnets are "well conceived and flowing
     limpidly."


1883 A   BOOKS - NONE

1883 B   SHORTER WRITINGS

1    ROBERTSON, ERIC S. "Chapter X. Christina G.
     Rossetti" in English Poetesses: A Series of
     Critical Biographies. London: Cassell, pp.
     338-48.
        A review of Goblin Market and Other Poems,
     The Prince's Progress and Other Poems, and A
     Pageant and Other Poems, which were printed
     and issued together by Roberts Brothers of
     Boston in 1882. Robertson describes "Goblin
     Market" and "The Prince's Progress" as "odd,
     and therefore original," but "hardly pleas-
     ant." Her strongest poems are her sonnets.
     He quotes "Dream Land," "A Farm Walk," "Re-

(ROBERTSON, ERIC S.)
member," "After Death," "Rest," and "Maude
Clare" in the remainder of the chapter.

2    SIMCOX, G. S.  Review of Letter and Spirit,
     Academy, XXIII (9 June), 395-96.
         Simcox discusses the structure of the book
     as "simple and ingenious.  Miss Rossetti
     takes the two Commandments on which all the
     law hangs, and then ranges the Commandments
     of each table in parallel order under them."
     She attains a "caustic shrewdness" and witti-
     ness in several places in the book.

3    SWINBURNE, ALGERNON CHARLES.  "Dedication to
     Christina Rossetti" in A Century of Roundels.
     London:  Chatto and Windus, v.
         In this poem Swinburne commemorates Chris-
     tina Rossetti's poetic genius.


1884 A   BOOKS - NONE

1884 B   SHORTER WRITINGS

1    SWINBURNE, ALGERNON CHARLES.  "A Ballad of Ap-
     peal.  To Christina Rossetti" in A Midsummer
     Holiday and Other Poems.  London:  Chatto and
     Windus, pp. 112-14.
         A lyrical poem of ten stanzas praising
     Christina Rossetti's poems as "sweet water
     from the well of song" (stanza 1).


1886 A   BOOKS - NONE

1886 B   SHORTER WRITINGS

1    ANON.  Review of Time Flies, Book Buyer (New

1886

(ANON.)
York), NS III (February), 27.
The reviewer praises the prose and verse
fragments as "full often of wise suggestion,
or furnishing themes of sober contemplation."

2    SHARP, WILLIAM. "The Rossettis. --Gabriele
Rossetti. --Maria Francesca Rossetti. --Dante
Gabriel Rossetti. --Wm. [sic] Michael
Rossetti. --Christina G. Rossetti," Fort-
nightly Review, XLV (1 March), 414-29.
Christina Rossetti is considered second only
to Elizabeth Browning. Christina Rossetti's
precocity is more notable than Dante
Gabriel's, evinced by the poems of her 1847
volume of poetry (entitled Verses and privately printed by her grandfather, Gaetano
Polidori). Sharp quotes "Vanity of Vanities,"
written by Christina Rossetti at the age of
sixteen.

3    ____. "The Rossettis. --Gabriele Rossetti.
--Maria Francesca Rossetti. --Dante Gabriel
Rossetti. --Wm. [sic] Michael Rossetti.
--Christina G. Rossetti," Living Age, CLXIX
(17 April), 161-70.
Reprint of 1886.B2.

4    ____. "The Rossettis. --Gabriele Rossetti.
--Mari Francesca Rossetti. --Dante Gabriel
Rossetti. --Wm. [sic] Michael Rossetti.
--Christina G. Rossetti," Eclectic Magazine,
CVI (May), 590-600.
Reprint of 1886.B2.

1887 A  BOOKS - NONE

## 1887 B    SHORTER WRITINGS

1   ANON. "Miss Rossetti's Poetry," London Quarter-
    ly Review, LXVIII (July), 338-50.
        A review of Goblin Market and Other Poems,
    The Prince's Progress and Other Poems, and A
    Pageant and Other Poems. Christina Rossetti's
    poems are characterized by simplicity, dig-
    nity, sincerity, and a sense of mystery.
    "'Goblin Market' is surely the most naïve and
    childlike poem in our language." To Chris-
    tina Rossetti nature is "always a relief, an
    escape." She has a "mystic and remote, yet
    homely and simple, genius."

2   GILCHRIST, HERBERT HARLAKENDEN. Anne Gilchrist:
    Her Life and Writings, With a Prefatory No-
    tice by William Michael Rossetti. London:
    T. Fisher Unwin, pp. 71, 145, 148, 160.
        Christina Rossetti is described as having a
    "sweetness, an unaffected simplicity and gen-
    tleness, with all her gifts that is very win-
    ning." Gilchrist quotes a letter in which
    Christina Rossetti offers a correction to
    Songs in a Cornfield, p. 71: "There should
    be no stop whatever after coil ('The green
    snake hid her coil'), but a colon after
    thickest in the next line."

3   STEDMAN, EDMUND CLARENCE. Victorian Poets, Re-
    vised and Extended by a Supplementary Chapter,
    to the Fiftieth Year of the Period Under Re-
    view. Boston: Houghton, Mifflin, pp. 280-81,
    443.
        "Miss Rossetti demands closer attention.
    She is a woman of genius, whose songs, hymns,
    ballads, and various lyrical pieces are stud-
    ied and original. I do not greatly admire her
    longer poems, which are more fantastic than

19

(STEDMAN, EDMUND CLARENCE)
imaginative; but elsewhere she is a poet of a
profound and serious cast, whose lips part
with the breathing of a fervid spirit within.
She has no lack of matter to express; it is
that expression wherein others are so fluent
and adroit which fails to serve her purpose
quickly; but when, at last, she beats her music out, it has mysterious and soul-felt meaning." Stedman notes: "Of women poets, Miss
Rossetti still finds none beside her on the
heights of spiritual vision. The fanciful
Masque of the Months, in A Pageant and Other
Poems, strengthens belief that her genius is
less visible through such constructions than
in brief, impassioned lyrics--stanzas like
'Passing and Glassing,'--and her sonnets, of
which the series entitled 'Later Life' is a
complement to that on Love in an early
volume."

1888 A   BOOKS - NONE

1888 B   SHORTER WRITINGS

1      BOWKER, R. R.  "London as a Literary Centre,"
       Harper's New Monthly Magazine, LXXVI (May),
       815-44.
          Christina Rossetti's contributions to the
       literary scene are described on pp. 827-28;
       her "deeply spiritual poems are known even
       more widely than those of her more famous
       brother, Dante Gabriel Rossetti." Bowker be-
       lieves Christina Rossetti's Goblin Market vol-
       ume exhibits "weird mysticism and singular
       sweetness."

2      LEVY, AMY.  "The Poetry of Christina Rossetti,"
       Woman's World (London), I (February), 178-80.

(LEVY, AMY)
A description of Christina Rossetti's volumes of poetry is followed by a "verdict" that
"Christina Rossetti stands alone, as Dante
Gabriel Rossetti stood alone. From the
branches of a wondrous tree, transplanted by
chance to our clime, we pluck the rare, exotic
fruit, and the unfamiliar flavour is very
sweet."

<u>1889 A</u>   BOOKS - NONE

<u>1889 B</u>   SHORTER WRITINGS

1      WALKER, JOHN. "The Lyrics of Miss Rossetti,"
<u>Manchester Quarterly, A Journal of Literature</u>
<u>and Art</u> (October), 393-404.
This article praises Christina Rossetti's
poetry for its clarity of style, its originality, and its perfect form. Walker quotes at
length various of his favorite poems, in an
effort to encourage greater recognition of
"her undoubted genius."

2      _____. <u>The Lyrics of Miss Rossetti</u>. Manchester:
Heywood. 12 pp.
Reprint of 1889.B1.


<u>1890 A</u>   BOOKS - NONE

<u>1890 B</u>   SHORTER WRITINGS

1      ANON. Review of <u>Poems</u>, <u>Literary World</u> (London),
NS XLIII (30 January), 100.
The paragraph on Christina Rossetti's book
contains excerpts from "Monna Innominata," and
the reviewer notes with pleasure the appearance of this collection of her poems.

2    BARZIA, ELSPETH H.  "A Group of Eminent Women.
     III. --Christina Rossetti," Sunday (June),
     615-18.
        A description of the unusually talented
     Rossettis is followed by a discussion of
     Christina Rossetti's poetry.  Christina
     Rossetti ranks "second only to Mrs. Barrett
     Browning."  Barzia quotes "Vanity of Vanities"
     and gives an account of Christina Rossetti's
     activities in connection with The Germ.
     Christina Rossetti's most original work is to
     be found in her sonnets.  The article closes
     with a quotation from "perhaps the greatest
     of all her poems," "Today for Me."


1891 A   BOOKS - NONE

1891 B   SHORTER WRITINGS

1    EWING, THOMAS J.  "Paraphrase of Poem Wanted,"
     N&Q, XII (15 August), 135-36; (19 September),
     234-35; (24 October), 337; (7 November),
     371-2; (28 November), 433.
        These five notes concern the accuracy of
     the phrase "watered shoot" in the poem "A
     Birthday."  Ewing thinks the poem is correct,
     in reply to the alternate suggestion that it
     should read "water-shoot."

2    LE GALLIENNE, RICHARD.  Review of Poems, Academy,
     XXXIX (7 February), 130-31.
        Christina Rossetti is "our one imaginative
     descendant of the magician of 'Kubla Khan.'"
     She has the "power of dream," the "gift of the
     child's imagination," in her verse; the "same
     strain of mystic materialism" of "The Blessed
     Damozel" is seen in some of her poetry.
     Rarely, she descends into the commonplace, and
     displays an admirably wide range of theme.

3    NOBLE, JAMES ASHCROFT.  "Christina Rossetti,"
     Literary Opinion (December), 155-57.
         Noble feels that Christina Rossetti's poet-
     ry is as fresh and unstrained as is that of
     William Blake.  She is described as a "true
     mystic, to whom each simple thing of nature
     . . . tells its own secret of meaning."
     Noble compares Christina Rossetti's devotion-
     al poetry to that of Herbert and Vaughan.  He
     concludes that the poems dealing with the
     inner life offer a "searching penetration of
     spiritual vision."


1892 A   BOOKS - NONE

1892 B   SHORTER WRITINGS

1    ANON.  Review of The Face of the Deep, The Inde-
     pendent, XLIV (27 October), 1524.
         The volume is praised for its poetry:  "It
     is not a book of deep spiritual penetration.
     But for lofty flights and soaring far and
     away into the depths of adoring contemplation
     we have seen nothing like this last book of
     Christina Rossetti."


1893 A   BOOKS - NONE

1893 B   SHORTER WRITINGS

1    ANON.  "Miss Rossetti's 'Verses,'" Speaker, VIII
     (25 November), 588.
         The review praises Christina Rossetti for
     keeping the standard of Christ aloft.  "Miss
     Rossetti owns not only the highest aim, but
     the clearest vision and the most delectable
     voice in modern poetry. . . .  She has a dic-

(ANON.)
tion as clear as glass, and a most rare and
distinguished music in her metres."

2    ANON.  Review of The Face of the Deep, The Inde-
pendent, XLV (12 January), 54.
This review discusses some of the 200 poems
of the volume.  "These remarkable religious
poems have the quaintness of Dr. Donne or the
holy Herbert, but more directness than they."
Many of the poems should be set to music despite their unusual meter.  The review quotes
four of the poems.

3    ANON.  Review of Poems, Edinburgh Review,
CLXXVIII (October), 494-95.
This review contains a note that "Goblin
Market" is below the level of some of Jean
Ingelow's poems because there is "an element
of the grotesque and the disproportionate in
it, and the two girls, like the figures in
Dante Rossetti's pictures, are unhuman and
unreal."

4    ANON.  Review of Verses, Athenaeum, No. 3451
(16 December), 842-43.
After describing the organization of the
book, the reviewer notes that it can be read
"without the more or less agreeable interrup-
tion of the edifying prose."  The poems, while
not equal to some of her earlier work, nevertheless are "satisfying" and "adequate."  Her
writing shows the "solemn curiosity" of Donne,
the felicity of Shelley, and the simplicity of
Verlaine.  "It is herself, really, that she
puts into these poems, her deepest self."

5    GOSSE, EDMUND.  "Christina Rossetti," Century
Magazine, XLVI (June), 211-17.

(EDMUND GOSSE)
"What is very interesting in her poetry is
the union of this fixed religious faith with
a hold upon physical beauty and the richer
parts of Nature which allies her with her
brother and with their younger friends." Of
"Goblin Market" Gosse writes: "I confess
that while I dimly perceive the underlying
theme to be a didactic one, and nothing less
than the sacrifice of self by a sister to re-
cuperate a sister's virtue, I cannot follow
the parable through all its delicious epi-
sodes. Like a Japanese work of art, again,
one perceives the general intention, and one
is satisfied with the beauty of all the detail, without comprehending or wishing to com-
prehend every part of the execution." Later
on he notes, "To find her exact parallel it
is at once her strength and her snare that we
must go back to the middle of the seventeenth
century. She is the sister of George Herbert;
she is of the family of Crashaw, of Vaughan,
of Wither."

6    HINKSON, KATHARINE (TYNAN). "The Poetry of
        Christina Rossetti," Bookman (London), V
        (December), 78-79.
        In this brief article Hinkson describes
     Christina Rossetti's self-willed seclusion and
     praises her religious poetry in Verses (1893)
     as well as the sonnets of A Pageant (1881).


1894 A   BOOKS - NONE

1894 B   SHORTER WRITINGS

1    CHAMBERS, EDMUND K.   Review of Verses, Academy,
        XLV (24 February), 162-64.

(CHAMBERS, EDMUND K.)
Chambers describes the book as a "singular-
ly beautiful volume." A veil of unearthli-
ness and detachment extends over all of her
poetry in this volume. Love means "not cling-
ing but charity." He discusses the Italian
influences on her poetry, her skillful use of
images and metrical forms, and her "low-
toned" concept of Christianity, with its bitterness, disappointments, and quiet optimism.

2    WATSON, LILY. "Christina Rossetti," Sunday at
Home, No. 2088 (5 May), 425-28.
A review of Verses. Watson reviews the book
by its eight divisions, describing and praising each in turn. "There is a wonderful mystical charm about the work of Christina
Rossetti; a simplicity combined with an intensity of passion that holds the reader spell-
bound. The flame of her genius burns like
the flame in Dante's 'Purgatorio'. . . ."

1895 A  BOOKS

1    NASH, JOSEPH JOHN GLENDINNING. A Memorial Sermon Preached at Christ Church, Woburn Square,
for the Late Christina Georgina Rossetti.
London: Skeffington. 24 pp.
The sermon is based on Proverbs, 31:31,
"Give her of the fruit of her hands, and let
her works praise her in the gates."

2    PROCTOR, ELLEN A. A Brief Memoir of Christina G.
Rossetti, With a Preface by W. M. Rossetti.
London: Society for the Promotion of Chris-
tian Knowledge. 85 pp.
Proctor gives a brief description of Chris-
tina Rossetti's home, family, and favorite

(PROCTOR, ELLEN A.)
   works of literature, such as the operatic
   poems of Metastasio; Hamlet; the writings of
   Scott, Byron, and Burns; Pope's "Iliad";
   Ariosto's Orlando Furioso; Goethe's Faust;
   Carleton's Traits and Stories of the Irish
   Peasantry; Maria Edgeworth's novels; Peter
   Parley's books; The Arabian Nights; Robinson
   Crusoe; "The Ballad of Chevy Chase"; and "Jack
   the Giant Killer." A description of Christina
   Rossetti's volumes of poetry and prose is fol-
   lowed by excerpts from some of her letters to
   Proctor.

1895 B   SHORTER WRITINGS

   1     ANON. "Christina Georgina Rossetti," Critic (New
         York), XXVI (12 January), 21.
            This brief article places Christina Rossetti
         within the great Romantic movement of the mid-
         dle third of the century. On p. 34 of this
         issue is a full-page reproduction of a crayon
         drawing of Christina done by Dante Gabriel
         Rossetti.

   2     ANON. "Christina Georgina Rossetti," Dial, XVIII
         (16 January), 37-39.
            This article enumerates Christina Rossetti's
         volumes of poetry and places her in a class
         shared only by Elizabeth Browning. Chris-
         tina Rossetti's secular poems are compared to
         some of Dante Gabriel's poems, as well as to
         several of Swinburne's poems. The author
         places Christina Rossetti's devotional poetry
         above that of Keble, Herbert, Newman, and
         Vaughan.

   3     ANON. "Christina Rossetti," SatR, LXXIX (5 Janu-
         ary), 5-6.

(ANON.)
The writer mourns the loss of a great modern poetess. He praises her poetry for its artistic finish, its intense, expressive simplicity, and its richness of sentiment.

4    ANON. "The Death of Christina Rossetti," Public Opinion, XVIII (10 January), 43.
The writer describes Christina Rossetti as a poet of rare lyrical gifts, and gives a short sketch of her life. He wonders how long her fame will last outside of the anthologies, "where she must always have a place."

5    ANON. "The Late Miss Rossetti," [London] Times (7 January), 7, col. 4.
This is a description of the service at which J. J. Glendinning Nash delivered a sermon in memory of Christina Rossetti. "Some critics had said that Miss Rossetti's poetry ranked next to that of the late Poet Laureate, and her religious poems could certainly be classed with the best examples of religious verse."

6    ANON. Obituary, [London] Times (3 January), 7, col. 6.
This is a paragraph noting the time and place of Christina Rossetti's funeral.

7    ANON. "Obituary. Christina Rossetti," Academy, XLVII (5 January), 12.
This obituary gives an incomplete list of Christina Rossetti's poetical works. "The similarity to her brother's poetry, in weirdness of imagination and in pictorial minuteness, has often been pointed out." She possesses spontaneity, which Dante Gabriel lacks, and the technique in her best work is compa-

1895

(ANON.)
   rable to that of Shelley, Tennyson, and
   Swinburne.

8    ANON. "Obituary. Miss Christina Rossetti,"
        [London] Times (1 January), 4, col. 3.
        A brief sketch of the Rossetti family is
        followed by a list of Christina Rossetti's
        major volumes of poetry and prose. "Her
        death leaves a distinct gap in the poetic lit-
        erature of the time."

9    ANON. "The Rambler," Book Buyer, XII (February),
        21-23.
        Christina Rossetti's "poetic vision had all
        the glow and delicacy of invention which ani-
        mates the canvas of the English pre-
        Raphaelite."

10   ANON. "Tributes to Miss Rossetti," Dial, XVIII
        (1 February), 69-70.
        This brief notice gives the time and place
        of Christina Rossetti's funeral, and quotes
        from eulogies published in Literary World,
        Academy, Athenaeum, and SatR.

11   BATES, KATHERINE LEE. "The Passing of Chirstina
        [sic] Rossetti," Dial, XVIII (1 March), 135.
        This is a four-stanza poem commemorating
        Christina Rossetti's death.

12   BELL, MACKENZIE. "Christina G. Rossetti," The
        Author (March), 269-70.
        This is a memorial to "one of the most lov-
        able women who ever lived." Bell notes that
        "the critic of the far future, of whom we
        hear so much and think so little, will accord
        a high place among the great poets of the cen-
        tury to the poet to whom we owe 'Amor Mundi,'

(BELL, MACKENZIE)
'An Apple Gathering,' 'Maude Clare,' 'The
Convent Threshold,' and 'Maiden-Song.'"

13 _____. "To Christina G. Rossetti (Greater as a
Woman than even as a Poet)," Literary World,
NS LI (4 January), 21.
The memorial verses read as follows:
I marvel not that God hath called away
    Thy peerless soul to where His saints abide;
Rather I praise Him that He bade thee stay
    On earth to be so long a heavenward guide.
                        (Dec. 30)

14 BENSON, ARTHUR CHRISTOPHER. "Christina
Rossetti," National Review, XXIV (February),
753-63.
Christina Rossetti is successful in the
world of dreamland and fantasy. Benson quotes
"Noble Sisters" as an exquisite example of the
modern ballad. The essay moves from a discussion of Christina Rossetti's early love
poetry, such as "A Birthday" and "Remember,"
to her religious poems, particularly "A Better
Resurrection," and closes with a comment on
the "shapeless prose" of The Face of the
Deep.

15 _____. "Christina Rossetti," Living Age, CCIV
(9 March), 620-26.
Reprint of 1895.B14.

16 COLERIDGE, CHRISTABEL R. "The Poetry of Christina Rossetti," Monthly Packet, LXXXIX
(March), 276-82.
This article gives a description of Christina Rossetti's devotional works, prose and
poetry. Christina Rossetti "loved all the old

(COLERIDGE, CHRISTABEL R.)
imagery of harp and crown, halo and palm
branch, wings and white garments, which, in
weaker hands, is apt to sink to the level of
the conventional prettiness of a Christmas
card.  In hers it fits itself to the needs of
a complex and uncommon devotion.  Her writing
is at one time pessimistic, morbid, and de-
sponding; at another, it rings with a trium-
phant note of Christian hopefulness."

17    GOSSE, EDMUND.  "Introduction" in Victorian
Songs: Lyrics of the Affections and Nature,
Collected and Illustrated by Edmund D.
Garrett.  Boston:  Little, Brown, pp. xxxii-
xxxiii.
Gosse praises Christina Rossetti for her
"beautiful direct simplicity" and "jets of
pure emotional melody which compare to ad-
vantage with the most perfect specimens of
Greek and Elizabethan song."  The selections
by Christina Rossetti are "Song" ("When I am
dead, my dearest"), "Song" (O roses for the
flush of youth"), "Song" ("Two doves upon the
self-same branch"), and "Three Seasons" (pp.
186-90).

18    HINKSON, KATHARINE TYNAN.  "London Letter,"
Literary World (Boston), XXVI (26 January),
24.
Hinkson describes her visit to the home of
Christina Rossetti and her mother in 1886.

19    _____.  "Some Reminiscences of Christina
Rossetti," Bookman (New York), I (February),
28-29.
This records the visit Hinkson had with
Christina Rossetti in 1885, describing Christina Rossetti's mother (who died the following year), and notes Christina Rossetti's

(HINKSON, KATHARINE TYNAN)
fondness for Cranford. Hinkson quotes a letter of 1888 in which Christina Rossetti
writes, "'I am not strong, and I am more than
content not to be strong.'"

20    _____. "Some Reminiscences of Christina
Rossetti," Bookman (London), VII (February),
141-42.
Reprint of 1895.B19.

21    JAPP, ALEXANDER H. "Two Pairs of Modern Poets.
By One Who Knows Them," Cassell's Family Magazine, XII (February), 223-27.
Japp discusses Lewis Morris, Austin Dobson,
Jean Ingelow, and Christina Rossetti. He
describes the detached, mystical, spiritual
tone characterizing much of Christina
Rossetti's poetry. "Over all she touches
there is the veil as of something spiritual,
. . . a kind of refined ghost world. . . ."

22    JOHNSON, M. "Christina G. Rossetti," Primitive
Methodist Quarterly Review, XXXVII (July),
469-81.
A brief account of Christina Rossetti's
life is followed by a description of the
major volumes of poetry and a criticism of
such prose works as Commonplace, which are
"chiefly of interest as the work of a distinguished woman-poet." Johnson considers
"Amor Mundi" to be Christina Rossetti's masterpiece. "It may indeed be said of her work
generally that her strength as an artist is
not so much in mastery over rhythm, or even
over the verbal texture of poetry, as in the
skill with which she expresses an allegorical
intent by subtle suggestion." Johnson concludes by classing Christina Rossetti among

CHRISTINA ROSSETTI: A REFERENCE GUIDE

1895

(JOHNSON, M.)
the greatest of the devotional poets and by
praising her sonnets.

23  LANG, ANDREW. "The Month in England," Cosmopol-
itan Magazine (London), XIX (June), 112.
Lang judges Christina Rossetti's poetry to
be equal to Mrs. Browning's. "Things of Miss
Rossetti's will live, with things of Carew's
and Suckling's."

24  LAW, ALICE. "The Poetry of Christina G.
Rossetti," Westminster Review, CXLIII (April),
444-53.
The keynote of Christina Rossetti's "word-
music" is "aesthetic mysticism and rich melancholy" associated with the Pre-Raphaelites.
"Consciously or unconsciously she is her own
mediaeval heroine. . . ." As with the Pre-
Raphaelite heroines, "the earthly love . . .
found an outlet in religious ecstasy," as
seen in Christina Rossetti's poem "Twice."
This leads to an estrangement from material
things.

25  MEYNELL, ALICE. "Christina Rossetti," New Review, XII (February), 201-6.
Christina Rossetti approaches the best beauties of poetry from the side of poetry rather
than from the side of the commonplace. Meynell discusses the subtleties of the meter
and some of Christina Rossetti's lines, ac-
knowledging her to be "poet and saint." "She
proves herself an artist, a possessor of the
weighty matters of the law of art, despite the
characteristic carelessness with which she
played by ear." The article closes with an
analysis of the techniques of "Amor Mundi" and
"The Prince's Progress."

33

1895

26    MEYNELL, ALICE. "Christina Rossetti," Living
      Age, CCIV (2 March), 569-72.
      Reprint of 1895.B25.

27    NOBLE, JAMES ASHCROFT. "The Burden of Christina
      Rossetti" in Impressions and Memories. Lon-
      don: Dent, pp. 55-64.
      Reprint of 1891.B3.

28    ROSSETTI, DANTE GABRIEL. Letters to Christina
      Rossetti in Dante Gabriel Rossetti: His Fam-
      ily-Letters, With a Memoir, ed. William
      Michael Rossetti. 2 vols. London: Ellis
      and Elvey, II, 224, 323.
          In a letter dated Wednesday, 23 March 1870,
      Dante Gabriel writes to his sister Christina
      Rossetti: "It [Commonplace] certainly is not
      dangerously exciting to the nervous system,
      but it is far from being dull for all
      that. . . .  P.S.--Of course I think your
      proper business is to write poetry, and not
      Commonplaces." In a letter of 3 December 1875
      he praises "Amor Mundi" as one of Christina
      Rossetti's "choicest masterpieces," but her
      "No Thank You, John" has the taint of the
      "modern vicious style."

29    ROSSETTI, WILLIAM MICHAEL, ed. Dante Gabriel
      Rossetti: His Family-Letters, With a Memoir.
      2 vols. London: Ellis and Elvey.
          According to William (I, 138), the rumor
      that Christina Rossetti was called "the Queen
      of the Praeraphaelites" was "a mere invention"
      put forth by Sara A. Tooley. William alludes
      to Christina Rossetti's habit of burning "huge
      bundles of letters" (I, 342), as did her
      brother Dante Gabriel. "The Chinaman," writ-
      ten when Christina Rossetti was eleven or
      twelve years old, is quoted (I, 79).

30    SHARP, WILLIAM. "Some Reminiscences of Chris-
      tina Rossetti," Atlantic Monthly, LXXV (June),
      736-49.
         This essay describes Sharp's initial meet-
      ing with Christina Rossetti in 1880, and
      gives an account of Christina Rossetti's
      childhood and her lifelong devotion to her
      mother. He quotes from four letters written
      to him in 1884-1886. He contrasts Christina
      Rossetti's dislike of Mariolatry, which in
      her opinion marred the Catholic Church, with
      Dante Gabriel's attraction to the worship of
      Mary. He concludes with a description of her
      care for Dante Gabriel in his last years be-
      fore her own terminal illness in 1894.

31    SMELLIE, A. "Christina Rossetti and Her Mes-
      sage," Wesleyan Methodist Magazine, CXVIII,
      203-6.
         This mourns the loss and praises the poetry
      of "one of the sweetest singers of our time."

32    SUTHERLAND, D. "Christina Rossetti," Literary
      World (Boston), XXVI (9 February), 40.
         Sutherland mourns the loss of a great teach-
      er and spiritual guide.

33    SWINBURNE, ALGERNON CHARLES. "A New Year's Eve:
      Christina Rossetti Died December 29, 1894,"
      Nineteenth Century, XXXVII (February), 367-68.
         This is a poem commemorating Christina
      Rossetti's death.

34    WATSON, LILY. "Christina G. Rossetti," Leisure
      Hour, XLIV (February), 245-48.
         After a brief biographical sketch, Watson
      states, "She seldom falls far below her own
      standard. The reader has not to plod wearily
      over vast tracts of dull, uninspired

1895

(WATSON, LILY)
work. . . . In this she may compare favour-
ably with Wordsworth." Poems (1890) is described, and the article closes with quotations from "Echo," "Dream Love," and "Up-Hill."

35   WATTS-DUNTON, THEODORE.  "Reminiscences of
Christina Rossetti," Nineteenth Century,
XXXVII (February), 355-66.
The author describes his first meeting with
Christina Rossetti and tells how she nursed
Dante Gabriel through illness.  He recounts
her love of nature which was evident to him
in their strolls about the garden at Cheyne
Walk.

36   _____.  "Christina Georgina Rossetti," Athenaeum,
No. 3506 (5 January), 16-18.
Watts-Dunton tells when and of what illness
Christina Rossetti died, and gives a descrip-
tion of her life and family.  He considers
her masterpiece to be "Amor Mundi."

37   _____.  "Christina Rossetti:  The Two Christmas-
tides," Athenaeum, No. 3507 (12 January), 49.
This two-stanza poem laments Christina
Rossetti's death.

1896 A   BOOKS - NONE

1896 B   SHORTER WRITINGS

1   ANON.  "Miss Rossetti's Last Volume," Spectator,
LXXVI (29 February), 309-10.
A review of New Poems.  The reviewer notes
the divergence between Christina Rossetti's
and Dante Gabriel's poetry.  The juvenile
poems at the end of the volume show the "un-

36

1896

(ANON.)
mistakeable [sic] promise of the future poetess." He concludes with a quotation of "A
Chilly Night."

2    ANON. "Miss Rossetti's Poems," SatR, LXXXI
(February), 194-97.
The reviewer finds interesting the poem
"Introspective" and admits that even the fail-
ures of a genius are interesting, such as "In
Progress," which is a "remarkable study of a
soul." The best poems of this volume are
among those in the devotional section.

3    ANON. "New Poems by Christina Rossetti," Literary World, Boston, XXVII (21 March), 85.
"This volume contains much which will be
most welcome to Christina Rossetti's admirers,
as some of the poems for the first time published are as beautiful as anything she ever
wrote, and the general average of the book is
very high." The reviewer notes of Christina
Rossetti that "endurance was the most cheerful
word in her vocabulary."

4    ANON. Notice of Maude: Prose and Verse, Bookman
(London), XI (December), 57.
This is a notice that James Bowden will publish Maude. The interest lies in the fact
that Maude contains the embryo of poems and
ideas afterwards worked out more fully in
other books.

5    ANON. Review of New Poems, Atlantic Monthly,
LXXVII (April), 570-71.
"It can scarcely be expected that her work
will ever be largely popular, yet it contains
just that bouquet of religion which is so rare
in Protestant poetry, and so grateful to those

37

1896

(ANON.)
    who have otherwise to content themselves with
    the few really beautiful hymns."

6   ANON. Review of New Poems, Edinburgh Review,
        CLXXXIII (April), 514.
        The reviewer finds "Look on This Picture"
    to be the most noteworthy poem of the volume,
    but there is nothing here equal to the best
    of what has already been published.

7   ANON. Review of New Poems, Guardian (London),
        LI (18 March), 432.
        The reviewer finds the volume repetitious
    and superfluous, and suggests that a possible
    reason for Christina Rossetti's refusal to
    publish some of the poems was her heavy bor-
    rowing of ideas from previous poets, as seen
    in "Repining" and "Helen Grey." He concludes,
    however, by welcoming the volume for exhibit-
    ing Christina Rossetti's "pure sincerity of
    feeling and expression" and William's excel-
    lent notes.

8   ANON. Review of Poems, London Quarterly Review,
        LXXXVII (October), 2-16.
        The writer gives a description of Poems, as
    well as New Poems and Verses. He concludes
    with a description of the Rossetti household.

9   ANON. Review of New Poems, Nation (New York),
        LXII (4 June), 436.
        The "curious flavor" of "The Way of the
    World" is compared to the tone of some of the
    poems of Emily Dickinson.

10  BENSON, ARTHUR CHRISTOPHER. "Christina Rossetti"
        in Essays. New York: Macmillan, pp. 268-91.
        Reprint of 1895.B14.

# CHRISTINA ROSSETTI: A REFERENCE GUIDE

1896

11   FIELD, MICHAEL. "Original Verse. To Christina
     Rossetti," Academy, XLIX (4 April), 284.
       This is a sonnet written in praise of Chris-
     tina Rossetti.

12   GILCHRIST, GRACE. "Christina Rossetti," Good
     Words, XXXVII (December), 822-26.
       In describing Christina Rossetti's visit to
     her house, Grace Gilchrist reprints eight let-
     ters written by Christina Rossetti to Mrs.
     Gilbert (Grace's mother), in an effort to in-
     dicate that Christina Rossetti's life was not
     so secluded as is popularly believed.  Gil-
     christ quotes "After Death" as well as the
     closing lines from "The Convent Threshold,"
     and she praises Christina Rossetti's "entire
     spontaneity."

13   JOHNSON, LIONEL. "Literature:  Miss Rossetti
     and Mrs. Alexander," Academy, L (25 July),
     59-60.
       Johnson praises Christina Rossetti as
     "faultless in tone and taste. . . .  In her
     three hundred sacred poems we find all pos-
     sible tones of feeling and thought."

14   KENYON, JAMES BENJAMIN. "Dante Gabriel Rossetti
     and His Sister Christina," Methodist Review,
     LXXVIII, 743-53.
       "The poems of the brother and of the sister
     have very little in common except an underly-
     ing sensuousness of purpose and an almost fas-
     tidious sense of melody." Kenyon traces "the
     austere beauty of a chaste and nun-like spir-
     it" in such poems as "Another Spring" and
     "Song" ("When I am dead, my dearest").

15   NASH, JOSEPH JOHN GLENDINNING. "The Christina
     Rossetti Memorial," Critic (New York), XXVIII
     (16 May), 357.

(NASH, JOSEPH JOHN GLENDINNING)
This is a notice of the memorial, super-
vised by Sir Edward Burne-Jones, to be placed
in Christ Church, Woburn Square, where Christina Rossetti attended for nearly twenty
years.

16 _____. "The Christina Rossetti Memorial," Nation (New York), LXII (21 May), 394.
Reprint of 1896.B15.

17 PAYNE, W. M. Review of New Poems, Dial, XX
(1 April), 205-6.
Payne describes the collection of poems as
an "unspeakably precious and fragrant gift,"
illustrative of Christina Rossetti's "pre-
cocious" genius. He particularly likes "Life
Hidden" and "Whitsun Eve," and ranks Christina
Rossetti as "if not distinctly the first, as-
suredly not the second" among Englishwomen
poets.

18 [PORTER, C.] Review of New Poems, Poet-lore,
VIII (March), 149-50.
"Suppression is the secret and the blazon of
Christina Rossetti's work; and if out of suppression she had the unerring wit to shape so
well, what might she not have done if her
nun-like bonds had not shut out of the sun her
rich sensuous nature and her sprite-like
fancy?" In conclusion he quotes from "Bed of
Forget-me-nots," and also "A Triad."

19 SEAMAN, OWEN. "The Links of Love" in The Battle
of the Bays. New York: Lane, pp. 69-70.
This is a three-stanza poem parodying "A
Birthday."

CHRISTINA ROSSETTI: A REFERENCE GUIDE

20    WALKER, JOHN.  [ROWLAND THIRLMERE.]  "Vita
       Aeterna:  In Memoriam Christinae G. Rossetti,"
       Manchester Quarterly, XV (January, 39–45.
          This poem consists of ten sections which
       mourn Christina Rossetti's death.

21    [WATTS–DUNTON, THEODORE.]  Review of New Poems,
       Athenaeum, No. 3564 (15 February), 207–9.
          "In the volume before us, as in all her pre-
       viously published writings, we see at its best
       what Christianity is as the motive power of
       poetry."

1897 A   BOOKS – NONE

1897 B   SHORTER WRITINGS

1     GARNETT, RICHARD.  "Rossetti, Christina Georgina"
       in Dictionary of National Biography.  New
       York:  Macmillan, XLIX, 282–84.
          This article, describing Christina
       Rossetti's life and her volumes of poetry, is
       based on the "Memoirs and Letters of Dante
       Rossetti" and the miniature biography of Chris-
       tina Rossetti by Proctor (See 1895 A1).  Ex-
       cept for "Goblin Market" and a few sonnets and
       lyrics, "she is, like most poetesses, purely
       subjective, and in no respect creative."  This
       sets her below Elizabeth Browning.

2     HUBBARD, ELBERT.  "Christina Rossetti" in Little
       Journeys to the Homes of Famous Women.  New
       York:  Putnam, No. V, 145–72.
          Hubbard describes the Charlotte Street resi-
       dence of the Rossettis, the members of the
       Rossetti family, and some of Christina
       Rossetti's volumes of poetry.  "Christina had
       the faculty of seizing beautiful moments, ex-
       alted feelings, sublime emotions and working
       them up into limpid song. . . ." (p. 168).

3     SNOW, FLORENCE L.  "On First Reading Christina
       Rossetti," Midland Monthly, VII (February),
       120–27.

1897

(SNOW, FLORENCE L.)
Snow praises Christina Rossetti's poetry
for its beauty and simplicity, quoting "An
October Garden," which shows "the exaltation
of spirit that illumines the commonest
things." The article includes a facsimile of
the holograph fragment from Christina
Rossetti's rough draft of "A Pageant"; the
manuscript is now in the Iowa State Department
of History and Archives in Des Moines.

4    SYMONS, ARTHUR. "Christina Rossetti" in Studies
     in Two Literatures. London: Leonard
     Smithers, 135-49.
     Symons finds Christina Rossetti to be a su-
     perior poet to Elizabeth Browning; Christina
     Rossetti's only equal is Sappho. Hers is not
     "the soaring rapture of a Crashaw" nor "the
     dusty, daily pieties of George Herbert."
     Symons praises Christina Rossetti's ability
     to see beyond normal vision and to bewitch her
     readers with poems like "Goblin Market" and
     "The Prince's Progress."

1898 A   BOOKS

1    BELL, MACKENZIE. Christina Rossetti:  A Bio-
     graphical and Critical Study. London:  Hurst
     and Blackett; Boston:  Roberts Brothers.  xvi
     + 364 pp.
     This is the first major study of Christina
     Rossetti.  All succeeding biographies of
     Christina Rossetti depend to a greater or
     lesser extent upon Bell's work.  About two-
     thirds of the book is biographical, offering
     a detailed description of Christina Rossetti's
     life, utilizing many of her letters, and in-
     cluding most if not all of the well-known

1898

(BELL, MACKENZIE)

anecdotes about her. The book is dedicated
to William Michael Rossetti, who helped Bell
compose and organize the biography. Fre-
quently Bell alludes to William's wishes to
include a certain fact or detail in the book.
Reviewers blamed William for forcing Bell to
include much unessential detail in the biography, against which charge William defended
himself in the preface of The Poetical Works
by stating that the critics insisted "that
most of the things which they disliked in the
book had been foisted into it by me in a
spirit of dictation at once arrogant and ob-
tuse, and had by Mr. Bell been too tamely per-
mitted to appear. Both Mr. Bell and I had
reason to complain of these critics: Mr. Bell
for being falsely credited with a degree of
sheepish acquiescence which had tended to
spoil his book, and I for being falsely ar-
raigned of an offence not enacted by me but
invented by my censors, who thereupon abused
me for doing what I had not done, and for de-
fects of mind and character evidenced by the
imputed doing of it" (xi). James A. Kohl, in
his article "A Medical Comment on Christina
Rossetti" (SEE 1968 B3), reprints a note written by Godfrey Bilchett, stating that "'Bell
told me . . . that he gave so much prosaic
matter of Christina Rossetti's because he
wished to bring out her . . . absolutely prac-
tical everyday mind combined with the gift of
the visionary, artist & poet; & Bell said his
father had found the same combination in the
Italians in the Argentine.'"

Chapters VI through X are critical, dealing
with the general poems, devotional poems,
children's books and prose stories, and devotional prose, followed by a general assessment

43

1898

(BELL, MACKENZIE)
    of Christina Rossetti's work. A bibliography
    by J. P. Anderson and a list of portraits and
    photographs of Christina Rossetti conclude
    the study.
       The biographical section is thorough and
    sympathetic, being the official biography of
    Christina Rossetti by one who loved her, as
    Bell terms himself (p. 2). The critical chap-
    ters are largely composed of a detailed de-
    scription of each volume of poetry and prose,
    with generous quoting from the best of her
    work. The criticism does not attempt a psy-
    chological study or an explanation of the
    meaning of the mysterious love poems of the
    late fifties. Instead, Bell concentrates on
    the stylistic devices used in the poetry,
    such as the meter of "O Roses for the Flush of
    Youth" (p. 203). The final chapter is a sur-
    vey of remarks concerning Christina Rossetti
    made by her major critics. Mackenzie Bell's
    files, which include his correspondence with
    William Michael Rossetti, his holograph notes,
    the galleys of the first edition, and his
    notes and drafts for an expanded fifth edi-
    tion (which was never published), are in the
    Troxell Collection at the Princeton Univer-
    sity Library.

1898 B    SHORTER WRITINGS

    1      ANON. "Christina Rossetti," Literary World (Lon-
           don), NS LVII (21 January), 43-44.
              Christina Rossetti is described as "a child
           of song, of unselfishness, and of mercy to all
           created things. . . . It cannot be said that
           the Rossettis formed a clique of mutual ador-
           ers. Dante Gabriel had abundant admiration
           for the genius of his sister, but at times he

1898

(ANON.)
could be severe in his strictures, and he considered candour to be the truest shape of
kindness.  Christina's morbid strains tried
his patience not a little, witness his description of them as 'the skeletons of Christina's various closets.'  On another occasion
this frank brother deplored the 'falsetto-
muscularity' of the 'Barrett-Browning style'
of certain poems written by his sister."

2    ANON.  "A Memorial to Christina Rossetti," SatR,
     LXXXVI (5 November), 601.
        This brief obituary notice, signed "E. J.,"
     describes the ceremony held at Christ Church,
     Woburn Square, by the Bishop of Durham in
     memory of Christina Rossetti as a woman and
     poet.  The memorial consists of a "reredos in
     five panels, representing our Lord and the
     four Evangelists, painted in the more conven-
     tional manner of Burne-Jones."

3    ANON.  Review of Bell's Christina Rossetti,
     Athenaeum, No. 3665 (22 January), 109.
        "The main influences on Christina Rossetti's
     life were the characters of her parents. . . .
     The habit of mind which flew to allegory from
     every occurrence of daily life must have
     seemed sweet reasonableness to the child of a
     father who saw in Dante a Socialist and Lu-
     theran before his time. . . .  The ordinary
     reader, too, would wish to learn more of the
     mother who endowed Rossetti with the sound
     common sense which was his distinguishing
     mark, and from whom her daughters learnt that
     grim piety of the horsehair sofa period,
     which made one of them refuse to look at
     Blake's illustrations to the Book of Job."

1898

4    ANON. Review of Bell's <u>Christina Rossetti</u>,
     <u>Literature</u>, II (22 January), 66–68.
          Christina Rossetti is described as being
     "unique in our easy-going age, this heroic
     blend of the impassioned poet with the ec-
     static nun. . . ." With <u>Time Flies</u>, "one is
     reminded of the kind of things that Walter
     Pater, another shrouded spirit, used to say,
     when he unbent." In conclusion, Christina
     Rossetti "lives by certain verses which a
     single small book would contain, and in that
     confined space she lives magnificently. . . .
     In her great lyrics, such as 'Passing away,
     saith the world,' 'At Home,' 'A Birthday,' or
     'A Better Resurrection,' not a word is out of
     place, not a cadence neglected, and the brief
     poem rises with a <u>crescendo</u> of passion."

5    ANON. Review of Bell's <u>Christina Rossetti</u>, <u>Na-</u>
     <u>tion</u>, LXVI (7 April), 272–73.
          Christina Rossetti's "difference from Dante
     Gabriel was a very interesting one. His lib-
     eral use of mediaeval pieties in his paint-
     ings and poems was altogether sentimental and
     aesthetic. He believed nothing of the Roman
     Catholic doctrine or legend. But Christina
     pounced upon nothing in this field that was
     not her own as a sincere and vital part of
     her religious life." One may wonder "what
     poems Miss Rossetti would have given us if
     she had had Mrs. Browning's experience of
     full and satisfying love . . . and yet it is
     her sonnets which approach the region of their
     personal sentiment that are Miss Rossetti's
     most memorable and perfect things."

6    ANON. "The Rossettis. Brother and Sister,"
     <u>Literary World</u> (Boston), XXIX (5 February),
     41–42.

CHRISTINA ROSSETTI: A REFERENCE GUIDE

1898

(ANON.)
   Christina Rossetti is described as "a
gifted, brilliant, exceptional woman, well
named Christina."

7   GRISWOLD, HATTIE TYNG. "Christina Rossetti" in
    Personal Sketches of Recent Authors. Chicago:
    A. C. McClurg, pp. 281-97.
       This chapter describes the members of Chris-
    tina Rossetti's family and gives an account
    of her life, interspersed with commentary on
    some of Christina Rossetti's best-known poems.
    When we read "A Birthday" and "a few other
    brief and simple lays which she wrote, easily
    it seems, and naturally as a bird sings, we
    cannot but deplore the fact that they are so
    few, and that she lived in the strained and
    affected atmosphere of a mystical aestheti-
    cism, and sought so diligently for far-
    fetched imagery and artificial and morbid
    phases of thought. There are scarcely a hand-
    ful of her poems where she is content to de-
    velop the genuine pathos of which she is ca-
    pable, in a simple and unaffected manner."

8   NICOLL, W. ROBERTSON. [CLAUDIUS CLEAR.] "Chris-
    tina Rossetti," Bookman (New York), VII
    (March), 73-75.
       A short sketch of Christina Rossetti's life
    is given. She is described as "undoubtedly
    the great poetess of Catholic Christianity.
    No such treasury of sacred verse as her vol-
    ume, modestly entitled Verses, has been writ-
    ten since George Herbert."

9   _____. "Mr. Bell's 'Christina Rossetti,'" Book-
    man (London), XIII (February), 154.
       Of Christina Rossetti, Nicoll writes:
    "Christina Rossetti was a great poetess in

47

1898

(NICOLL, W. ROBERTSON)
almost all her moods.  Her own experience of
love and sorrow was of the deepest, and she
has given it permanent expression.  But she
was, above all things, a Christian of the
churchly type, and it is as an interpreter
of Christianity, or rather of this phase of
Christianity, that she will live.  Those who
are with her in her religious belief will,
without hesitation, pronounce her the greatest of English religious poets, greater than
Herbert or Vaughan or Crashaw, and they will
rest her claim mainly on her book entitled
'Verses.'  There is much reason to think that
she would have accepted this choice."


1899 A   BOOKS

1       WESTCOTT, BROOKE FOSS.  An Appreciation of the
        Late Christina G. Rossetti.  London:  Society
        for the Promotion of Christian Knowledge.   24
        pp.
            Westcott praises Christina Rossetti's poet-
        ic genius:  "simple and ordinary thoughts
        gain from the indescribable grace of her
        treatment a fresh coherence and dignity" (p.
        23).


1899 B   SHORTER WRITINGS

1       ANON.  "The Christina Rossetti Memorial.  Sir
        Edward Burne-Jones's Last Work," Magazine of
        Art, XXII, 88-90.
            The description of the memorial is accom-
        panied by two photographs, and the inscrip-
        tion is reprinted.  The memorial is located
        in Christ Church, where Christina Rossetti at-
        tended for nearly twenty years.

1899

2    ANON. "Panels in the Reredos in Christ Church,
Woburn Square, London. In Memorial of Christina Rossetti," Critic (New York), XXXIV
(January), 13.
     This is a picture of the last work of Ed-
ward Burne-Jones.

3    ANON. "Some Women Poets," Quarterly Review,
CLXXXIX (January), 32-57.
     The reviewer describes Christina Rossetti
as "restrained, direct and sincere." But "in
her life, as recorded by Mr. Mackenzie Bell,
we look in vain for traces of the poet soul
which dominates her published works." Christina Rossetti's poetry shows an austerity of
expression which sets her above Mrs. Browning,
whose poetry is tainted by "the emotional
impulse."

4    ANON. "Some Women Poets," Living Age, CCXXI
(1 April), 26-34, (8 April), 123-33.
Reprint of 1899.B3.

5    LIVINGSTON, LUTHER S. "The First Books of Some
English Authors. III. Dante Gabriel and
Christina G. Rossetti," Bookman (New York), X
(November), 245-47.
     Livingston describes the early poetry of
Christina Rossetti and Dante Gabriel printed
by their grandfather at his private press.
The first such volume by Christina Rossetti
was Verses, dedicated to her mother. Livingston reproduces the title page and reprints
the address to the reader written by Christina Rossetti's grandfather, Gaetano Polidori.

1900 A   BOOKS - NONE

1900

1900 B  SHORTER WRITINGS

1    CARY, ELISABETH LUTHER. "Christina Rossetti"
     and "Christina Rossetti: Her Poetry" in The
     Rossettis, Dante Gabriel and Christina. New
     York and London:  G. P. Putnam's Sons,
     228-75.
        The first chapter gives an account of
     Christina Rossetti's life. In the second
     chapter her volumes of poetry are described
     and her sonnets are praised for their fitness
     of form. The two great qualities of Chris-
     tina Rossetti's verse are "sincerity and fer-
     vour," but her prose leaves something to be
     desired.

2    McGILL, ANNA BLANCHE. "Some Famous Literary
     Clans:  I. The Rossettis," Book Buyer, XX
     (June), 378-82.
        This article contains pictures of Gabriele
     Rossetti, Rossetti's studio, and the dining-
     room at No. 16 Cheyne Walk. In the descrip-
     tion of the Rossetti family Christina Rossetti
     is characterized as "the slender girl . . .
     whose spiritual face, with its beautiful lips
     and lofty brow, was her brother's model for
     his earlier work. . . ."

3    WALKER, HUGH. "Christina Georgina Rossetti
     (1830-1894)" in The Age of Tennyson. Hand-
     books of English Literature. London:  Bell,
     pp. 244-46.
        Walker lists Christina Rossetti's publica-
     tions, and considers "Vanity of Vanities" to
     be her finest sonnet. She surpasses her
     brother in clarity of style. Walker believes
     that Elizabeth Browning is the finer of the
     two poets, although Christina Rossetti is more
     even in overall merit. Christina Rossetti's

1902

(WALKER, HUGH)
"fine simplicity" complements her brother's
"sonorous richness" of style.

## 1901 A   BOOKS - NONE

## 1901 B   SHORTER WRITINGS

1   BOASE, FREDERIC. "Rossetti, Christina Georgina"
   in Modern English Biography. Truro: Nether-
   ton and Worth, III, 306.
      Boase gives the important dates in Chris-
   tina Rossetti's life and lists several critical works about her.

2   KENYON, JAMES BENJAMIN. "Dante Gabriel Rossetti
   and His Sister Christina" in Loiterings in Old
   Fields: Literary Sketches. New York: Eaton,
   pp. 166-71.
   Reprint of 1896.B14.

3   THOMPSON, ALEXANDER HAMILTON. "Tennyson and the
   Victorian Poets" in A History of English Literature, and of the Chief English Writers,
   Founded upon the Manual of Thomas B. Shaw.
   London: John Murray, pp. 785-86.
      Christina Rossetti's "purely lyric gift was
   greater than her brother's, but she had not
   his complete mastery of divers [sic] kinds of
   music."

## 1902 A   BOOKS - NONE

## 1902 B   SHORTER WRITINGS

1   PAYNE, WILLIAM MORTON. "Christina Georgina
   Rossetti (1830-1894)" in Library of the
   World's Best Literature Ancient and Modern,

1902

(PAYNE, WILLIAM MORTON)
    ed. C. D. Warner. 46 vols. New York:   J. A.
Hill and Co., XXXI, 12397–99.
    Payne notes that Christina Rossetti had
"more exquisite perception of poetical form"
than Elizabeth Browning had.   There is a
brief account of Christina Rossetti's life
and a list of her most notable volumes of poetry.   The insistent characteristics of her
work are an "ardent mysticism" and "a certain
strain of pensive melancholy."


1903 A   BOOKS – NONE

1903 B   SHORTER WRITINGS

1     GOSSE, EDMUND.   "Christina Rossetti" in Critical
      Kit-Kats.   New York:   Dodd, Mead and Co., pp.
      135–62.
           The first part of the essay (pp. 135–57) is
      a reprint of 1893.B5.   The remainder is an
      obituary of Christina Rossetti's death.

2     ROSSETTI, WILLIAM MICHAEL.   Rossetti Papers,
      1862 to 1870: A Compilation.   New York:
      Charles Scribner's Sons.
           In letter No. 121 (p. 202), Christina
      Rossetti writes to William of the "worst mis-
      print of all" left uncorrected in The Prince's
      Progress and Other Poems.   As with The Family
      Letters, omissions are indicated by three
      dots, as in the diary entry of Tuesday, 8 June
      1869 (p. 396):   "Christina went off with the
      Scotts, to spend a month or more at
      Penkill. . . ."   Christina Rossetti is men-
      tioned throughout the volume, which contains
      fourteen of her letters.

1904 A  BOOKS - NONE

1904 B  SHORTER WRITINGS

1   ANON. "Art III. Christina Rossetti," Church
    Quarterly Review, LIX (October), 58-75.
        This review of The Poetical Works provides
    a brief biographical sketch of Christina
    Rossetti. The reviewer quotes from the best
    poems of the volume, and closes by quoting
    "Resurgam." He feels that the difference be-
    tween her devotional and her general poems is
    nominal, not essential.

2   ANON. "Books. Christina Rossetti's Poems,"
    Spectator, XCIII (9 July), 51-52.
        The reviewer discusses the merits of Chris-
    tina Rossetti's poetry, which are sincerity
    and spontaneity, as seen in such poems as
    "From House to Home." The best secular poem
    is "Goblin Market"; the best meditative poems
    are "The World," "Amor Mundi," and "Up-Hill."

3   ANON. "Literature. Christina Rossetti," TLS,
    No. 117 (8 April), 105-6.
        Christina Rossetti is like Matthew Arnold
    in her desire for "security of righteousness."
    Her despondence is likened to Shelley's, her
    happiness to Herbert's. "Indeed, in her poet-
    ry there is the long and quiet tragedy of a
    mind too aspiring and a body too frail for the
    conditions of our life. . . ."

4   ANON. "The Poems of Christina Rossetti," Bookman
    (London), XXVI (April), 31.
        "Curiously lucid, and persistently natural
    and restrained, she touches the reader as many
    greater poets are unable to do. A delicate
    timidity clings to everything she wrote."

1904

5    GOSSE, EDMUND. "Christina Georgina Rossetti" in
     English Literature: An Illustrated Record in
     Four Volumes. New York: Grosset and Dunlap,
     IV, 349-52.
        There is a brief account of Christina
     Rossetti's life, a facsimile of her manu-
     script of "Roses and Roses," and a list of
     the volumes of poetry published within her
     lifetime. A quotation of "Dream Land" and
     "Echo" closes the article.

6    HUEFFER, FORD MADOX. "The Collected Poems of
     Christina Rossetti," Fortnightly, NS LXXV
     (1 March), 393-405.
        Hueffer relates autobiographical events to
     Christina Rossetti's poetry and praises her
     for holding aloof from the problems of her
     day.

7    _____. "The Collected Poems of Christina
     Rossetti," Living Age, CCXLI (9 April),
     158-67.
     Reprint of 1904.B6.

8    MORE, PAUL ELMER. "Christina Rossetti," Atlantic
     Monthly, XCIV (December), 815-21.
        More describes Christina Rossetti's burden
     of unfulfilled affection and compares the mas-
     culine effect of intellectual play in the
     poems of Elizabeth Browning with the feminine
     harmony and passivity of Christina Rossetti's
     sonnets. Her verse of bitterness and suffer-
     ing, such as "The Lowest Room," is compared
     with some of James Thomson's lines from "City
     of Dreadful Night."

9    RALEIGH, WALTER. "Christina Rossetti" in
     Chambers's [sic] Cyclopaedia of English Liter-
     ature. 3 vols. London: W. and R. Chambers,
     Ltd., 1902-1904, III (1904), 646-48.

1904

(RALEIGH, WALTER)
    After providing a brief biographical sketch
Raleigh praises Christina Rossetti for the
sincerity and spontaneity of her poetry.  The
article concludes with the quotation of
"Shall I Forget?" "A Birthday," "Echo,"
"Rest," "Soeur Louise de la Miséricorde," and
one of the "Monna Innominata" sonnets.  The
essay includes a reproduction of Dante
Gabriel's 1877 crayon drawing of Christina
Rossetti and her mother.

10   ROSSETTI, WILLIAM MICHAEL.  "Memoir" in The Po-
     etical Works of Christina Georgina Rossetti.
     London:  Macmillan, xlv-lxxi.
        This short biographical essay gives a de-
     scription of Christina Rossetti's life and
     physical appearance, followed by a list of
     the portraits of her.  William offers a few
     conservative comments on Christina Rossetti's
     methods of composition, but prefers to remain
     silent as to the merit of her poetry, which
     speaks for itself.

11   _____.  "Preface" in Poems of Christina Rossetti
     (Golden Treasury Series), Chosen and Edited
     by William M. Rossetti.  London:  Macmillan
     and Co., pp. v-xiv.
        William states that the purpose of this
     book is to provide the reader with a selec-
     tion of Christina Rossetti's best poems.  He
     summarizes and comments upon such poems as
     "Goblin Market" and the "Monna Innominata"
     sonnets, and then discusses some of the most
     outstanding characteristics of Christina
     Rossetti's poetry, such as spontaneity, sin-
     cerity, and "an unceasing use of biblical dic-
     tion."  The preface is followed by "Extracts

1904

(ROSSETTI, WILLIAM MICHAEL)
from Reviews" (xv-xix).  The 332 pages of poetry contain 187 poems.

12    SWINBURNE, ALGERNON CHARLES.  "A New Year's Eve:
Christina Rossetti Died December 29, 1894" in
A Channel Passage and Other Poems.  London:
Chatto and Windus, pp. 112-14.
Reprint of 1895.B33.

1905 A   BOOKS - NONE

1905 B   SHORTER WRITINGS

1    HUNT, WILLIAM HOLMAN.  Pre-Raphaelitism and the
Pre-Raphaelite Brotherhood.  2 vols.  New
York:  Macmillan, I, 154; II, 87.
In describing a dinner engagement at the
Rossetti home, Hunt notes that Christina
Rossetti was "exactly the pure and docile-
hearted damsel that her brother portrayed
God's Virgin pre-elect to be."  He quotes
Christina Rossetti's sonnet on the Pre-Raphaelite Brotherhood.  "Gentle Christina Rossetti's
sonnet is an example of the tone of hostility
to the Academy prevalent in her circle from
the beginning.  This not only conveyed the
idea that the Institution was one to which re-
form in due time would be wholesome, but that
it was a power altogether destructive to the
true spirit of art, and one which it had been
our secret object to overthrow."

2    MORE, PAUL ELMER.  "Christina Rossetti" in Shel-
burne Essays:  Third Series.  New York:  G. P.
Putnam's Sons, pp. 124-42.
Reprint of 1904.B8.

3    REID, STUART J.  "In Memory of Christina
     Rossetti," Sunday Magazine, XXXIV (September),
     859-60.
          Reid gives a brief description of Christina
     Rossetti's life and family.  "Her mystical,
     impassioned, devotional poetry betrays many
     moods, and some of them are the reverse of
     buoyant, though all are quick with life.  In
     sheer lyrical strength and nervous beauty of
     expression, her best work has claims which
     can never be ignored. . . .  She did not so
     much possess religion, as was possesed by it."

4    WATSON, WILLIAM.  "To Christina Rossetti" in The
     Poems of William Watson.  2 vols.  New York:
     Lane, II, 107.
          This is a memorial poem praising Christina
     Rossetti's poetic genius.


1906 A   BOOKS - NONE

1906 B   SHORTER WRITINGS

1    AGRESTI-ROSSETTI, OLIVIA.  "Cristina Giorgina
     Rossetti," Nuova Antologia, CCVII (May),
     37-52.
          This article describes Christina Rossetti's
     home life and the members of her family, and
     then briefly examines her devotional poetry
     dealing with death, as well as her Italian
     sonnets.

2    ARMYTAGE, A. J. GREEN.  "C. G. Rossetti" in Maids
     of Honour.  London:  Blackwood, pp. 273-302.
          This chapter describes Christina Rossetti's
     family and gives an account of her life.
     Armytage notes the contrast between Christina

(ARMYTAGE, A. J. GREEN)
Rossetti's revulsion for Mariolatry and Dante
Gabriel's attraction to it.

3    GOYAU, L. FELIX-FAURE. "La Nostalgie d'une
     Conscience Exilée, Christina Rossetti" in
     Vers la Joie. Paris: Perrin, pp. 73-193.
       Goyau gives an account of Christina
     Rossetti's life, including descriptions of
     members of her family, her surroundings, and
     her love for Collinson and Cayley. He dis-
     cusses her religious mysticism, her Italian
     poems, her propensity for introspection and
     sadness, aloofness from the grand movements
     of her times, and her catholic spirit. "Sa
     poésie est ardente, pure et douloureuse . . .
     où l'on retrouve toujours l'écho des inspira-
     tions catholiques de sa race."

4    GRAPPE, GEORGES. "C. G. Rossetti" in Essai sur
     la Poésie Anglaise au XIXe Siècle. Paris:
     E. Sansot, pp. 57-59.
       Grappe notes the freshness and simplicity
     of the poems in Goblin Market and Other Poems
     and the monotony of much of her devotional
     verse.

5    ROSSETTI, WILLIAM MICHAEL. "Charles Cayley and
     Christina Rossetti" in Some Reminiscences of
     William Michael Rossetti. 2 vols. London:
     Brown Langham, II, 311-15.
       Cayley is described as a close, abstracted,
     and extremely unworldly scholar. He met
     Christina Rossetti when she was thirty-one,
     and by 1863 she was in love with him; she ad-
     mired him even after his agnosticism was
     known to her, but she could never marry him.

6    RUTHERFORD, MILDRED.  "Christina Rossetti" in
     English Authors:  A Hand-Book of English Lit-
     erature from Chaucer to Living Writers.
     Atlanta, Ga.:  Franklin, 631-33.
         This is a brief sketch of Christina
     Rossetti's life, based on Mackenzie Bell's
     biography.

7    WATTS-DUNTON, THEODORE.  "Christina Rossetti:
     The Two Christmastides" in The Coming of Love,
     Rhona Boswell's Story, and Other Poems.  Lon-
     don and New York:  Lane, pp. 253-55.
     Reprint of 1895.B37.


1907 A  BOOKS

1    BREME, MARY IGNATIA.  Christina Rossetti und der
     Einfluss der Bibel auf Ihre Dichtung:  Eine
     Literarisch-Stilistische Untersuchung,
     Münstersche Beiträge zur Englischen
     Literaturgeschichte, No. 4.  Münster:
     Schöningh.  xi + 96 pp.
         Part I of this published dissertation gives
     a brief account of Christina Rossetti's life
     and a list of her volumes of poetry.  In Parts
     II and III Breme presents a two-columned com-
     parison of some lines from Christina
     Rossetti's religious verse and corresponding
     Bible verses.  In Part IV she discusses the
     stylistic influences of the Bible on Christina
     Rossetti's work, comparing some lines of
     Christina Rossetti's devotional poetry with
     relevant Bible verses.

1907 B  SHORTER WRITINGS

1    SAINTSBURY, GEORGE EDWARD BATEMAN.  "Poetry Since
     the Middle of the Century" in A Short History

1907

    (SAINTSBURY, GEORGE EDWARD BATEMAN)
      of English Literature. New York: Macmillan,
      pp. 779-83.
        Christina Rossetti is discussed on pp.
      782-83. "Her pathos has never been surpassed,
      except in the great single strokes of Shake-
      speare and a very few other Elizabethans.
      But her most characteristic strain is where
      this pathos blends with, or passes into, the
      utterance of religious awe, unstained and un-
      weakened by any craven fear."

2    SYMONS, ARTHUR. "Christina G. Rossetti: 1830-
      1894" in The Poets and the Poetry of the Nine-
      teenth Century, ed. Alfred H. Miles. London:
      George Routledge; New York: E. P. Dutton, IX,
      1-16.
        The secret of Christina Rossetti's style is
      its "sincerity as the servant of a finely
      touched and exceptionally seeing nature." In
      her devotional poetry "she does not preach;
      she prays." Her poems show "finished workman-
      ship."

1908 A  BOOKS - NONE

1908 B  SHORTER WRITINGS

1    ANON. "Christina Rossetti, 1830-1894," Book News
      Monthly (Philadelphia), XXVI (January),
      369-72.
        This article gives a brief description of
      Christina Rossetti's life. "Christina
      Rossetti was not a poetic artist. She never
      conquered forms; it is doubtful if she ever
      tried. She had a message to give; she was a
      poet by instinct; she wrote as the verses came
      to her, and she rarely stopped to do much re-
      vising."

2    WYZEWA, T. de.  "Une Femme-Poète Anglaise:
     Christina Rossetti," Revue des Deux Mondes,
     XLVIII (15 December), 922-33.
          Wyzewa, in reviewing The Family Letters of
     Christina Georgina Rossetti, feels that the
     letters offer a vivid portrait of Christina
     Rossetti--her affection for her sister, for
     example, comes out clearly in several of the
     letters.  Many of the letters are beautifully
     written despite their trivial subject-matter,
     as with invitations, etc.


1909 A   BOOKS - NONE

1909 B   SHORTER WRITINGS

1    DUNBAR, OLIVIA HOWARD.  Review of The Family
     Letters of Christina Georgina Rossetti, North
     American Review, CLXXXIX (April), 618-21.
          Dunbar regards the letters as an important
     contribution to a total picture of Christina
     Rossetti and notes Christina Rossetti's ad-
     miration for Augusta Webster, as well as her
     lack of sympathy for "George Eliot as a bard."


1910 A   BOOKS - NONE

1910 B   SHORTER WRITINGS

1    CHAPMAN, EDWARD MORTIMER.  "The Doubters and the
     Mystics" in English Literature in Account with
     Religion, 1800-1900.  Boston:  Houghton
     Mifflin, pp. 446-48.
          Christina Rossetti's mysticism represents a
     "somewhat extreme form of the nineteenth-
     century type."  "Give Me the Lowest Place"
     savours "of exaggeration and of feeling

(CHAPMAN, EDWARD MORTIMER)
cultivated for its own sake; just as the
question and answer [in 'Up-Hill'] . . . seem
to overemphasize the sombre and unrelenting
features of experience."

2    MEYNELL, ALICE. "Introduction" in Poems by
Christina Rossetti, With Illustrations by
Florence Harrison. London: Blackie and Son,
pp. vii-x.
Meynell gives a brief biographical sketch,
followed by criticism of Christina Rossetti's
poetry. "In 'The Convent Threshold' there is,
I think, more passion than in any other poem
written by a woman." Among contemporary au-
thors which Christina Rossetti read are Canon
Dixon, Alfred Gurney, Mrs. Gaskell, Elizabeth
Barrett Browning, Adelaide Procter, and Jean
Ingelow. Meynell observes that because of
Christina Rossetti's constant meditation upon
death, "her portrait should have been painted
with the skull on the table."

3    SAINTSBURY, GEORGE. "The Prae-Raphaelite School"
in A History of English Prosody from the
Twelfth Century to the Present Day. London:
Macmillan, III, 352-59.
This article examines the meter of "Goblin
Market, described as a "dedoggerelised
Skeltonic," concluding that "the more the
metre is studied the more audacious may its
composition seem."

4    WALKER, HUGH. "The Turn of the Century: New Influences" in The Literature of the Victorian
Era. Cambridge, England: Cambridge University Press, pp. 501-8.
Walker feels that since religion was so much
a part of Christina Rossetti's being, her po-

(WALKER, HUGH)
etry is all of a piece and defies categorization. No one else of her generation can
match her fullness of faith. "No one else of
her fellow-poets in her generation has this
fulness of faith. Arnold seems to set aside
the idea of a second life as a mere dream;
Browning reaches it through an argument in
which the logic is not altogether flawless;
Tennyson faintly trusts the larger hope;
Dante Rossetti cares for none of these
things." Her poems on death are not gloomy,
for the grave offers rest and the life beyond
offers a happiness unknown in this life. He
notes the striking contrast between Christina
Rossetti's simple, limpid style and that of
her brother Dante Gabriel, which is often
"rich to gorgeousness."

1911 A   BOOKS - NONE

1911 B   SHORTER WRITINGS

1     Betham-Edwards, [Matilda Barbara.] "Tea with
       Christina Rossetti," in Friendly Faces of
       Three Nationalities. London: Chapman and
       Hall, pp. 129-35.
          This chapter describes an afternoon with
       Christina Rossetti in 1870, during which
       Christina Rossetti shocked Betham-Edwards by
       confessing that she had never seen the sun
       rise.

2     CAZAMIAN, MADELEINE. "Christina Rossetti,"
       Revue de Paris, XVIII (1 August), 575-89.
          After giving a brief biographical sketch,
       Cazamian compared Christina Rossetti's poetry
       to that of Keats. "The City of Death" is like

(CAZAMIAN, MADELEINE)
"Eve of St. Agnes" in its sensuous descrip-
tions.  Christina Rossetti has the reserve,
delicacy, and naïveté of a recluse.  The second half of the article deals with Christina
Rossetti's religious and metaphysical poetry,
as well as with the "persistance douloureuse"
of the meditative poems.  The poems of this
woman who was divided against herself remain
among the great works of the century.

3    HUEFFER, FORD MADOX.  "Christina Rossetti,"
     Fortnightly Review, XCV (March), 422-29.
       Hueffer calls Christina Rossetti "the
     greatest master of words" of the nineteenth
     century.  She is more modern a poet than her
     brother, "undergoing within herself always
     a fierce struggle between the pagan desire
     for life, for the light of the sun and love,
     and an asceticism that, in its almost more
     than Calvinistic restraint, reached also to
     a point of frenzy. . . .  And, since she
     suffered nearly always from intense physical
     pain and much isolation, there was little
     wonder that her poems were almost altogether
     introspective--just, indeed, as all modern
     poetry must be almost altogether intro-
     spective."

4    _____.  "Christina Rossetti and Pre-Raphaelite
     Love" in Ancient Lights.  London:  Chapman and
     Hall, pp. 54-69.
       This is a reprint of 1911.B3, with a note
     added at the end concerning Garnett's use of
     the word "morbid" when he describes Christina
     Rossetti's poetry in the Dictionary of Nation-
     al Biography (See 1897.B1).  When asked about
     his use of that word, Garnett "insisted that
     the word 'morbid' as applied to literature

1912

(HUEFFER, FORD MADOX)
signified that which was written by a person
suffering from disease. I [Hueffer] insisted
that it meant such writing as was calculated
to disease the mind of the reader."

5       _____. "Christina Rossetti and Pre-Raphaelite
Love" in Memories and Impressions: A Study
in Atmospheres. New York: Harper and
Brothers, pp. 60-77.
Reprint of 1911.B4.


1912 A   BOOKS - NONE

1912 B   SHORTER WRITINGS

1     ANON. "A Picture of Christina Rossetti," Poetry
Review, I (May), 241.
This paragraph recounts the description of
Christina Rossetti given by Mackenzie Bell at
the Putney meeting on April 10. ". . . her
impulse to write was spontaneous, it was not
derived even in the best sense from the
achievements of others."

2     DE BARY, ANNA BUNSTON. "The Poetry of Christina
Rossetti," Poetry Review, I (May), 203-10.
"Christina is never sensational, and yet
she brings a freshness to the most well-worn
themes." The characteristics of her poetry
are sincerity, music, grace, and variety in
uniformity.

3     O'BRIEN, MRS. WILLIAM. "Christina Rossetti" in
Unseen Friends. London: Longmans and Green,
pp. 435-63.
This chapter gives a short description of
Christina Rossetti's life and family. "To

1912

(O'BRIEN, MRS. WILLIAM)
those who are interested in literary profits,
it may be of interest to know that until 1862
she seldom made £10; from 1862 to 1890, her
brother tells us, she made £40 a year, less
rather than more. After 1890, her poetic
reputation was fully established, and her
gains increased, without ever being large."
There are quotations from five of the "Monna
Innominata" sonnets, as well as a few excerpts from letters by Dante Gabriel and
Christina Rossetti. This account is based
primarily on Bell and on William Michael
Rossetti's "Memoir."

4    SHARP, WILLIAM. "Some Reminiscences of Christina Rossetti" in Papers Critical and Reminiscent, Selected and Arranged by Mrs. William
Sharp. New York: Duffield, pp. 66-103.
Reprint of 1895.B30.

5    TYNAN, KATHARINE. "Santa Christina," Supplement
to Bookman (London), XLI (January), 185-90.
This article describes Tynan's admiration
for and friendship with Christina Rossetti and
Dante Gabriel. The Bookman text contains
eight illustrations as well as facsimiles of
Christina Rossetti's manuscript of "To My
Mother on Her Birthday" and her manuscript of
"Sleeping at Last."

6    _____. "Santa Christina," Living Age, CCLXXII
(17 February), 431-36.
Reprint of 1912.B5.


1913 A   BOOKS - NONE

1913 B    SHORTER WRITINGS

1    BURKE, CHARLES BELL. "Sketch of Christina
     Rossetti" in Selected Poems of Christina G.
     Rossetti. New York: Macmillan, pp. xix-lxiv.
         This introduction describes Christina
     Rossetti's life and family, based on accounts
     by Mackenzie Bell, Harry Buxton Forman, and
     Edmund Gosse. "Critical Estimates," which
     follows, contains excerpts from a number of
     articles about Christina Rossetti.

2    LOWTHER, GEORGE. "Christina Rossetti," Contempo-
     rary Review, CIV (November), 681-89.
         Lowther describes various elements of Chris-
     tina Rossetti's poetry, such as the "myster-
     ies of the Christian faith"; except for the
     uncharacteristic "Goblin Market," her poems
     "are almost entirely untouched by Pre-
     Raphaelitism. Their prevalent quality is in-
     tensity." He notes the mournful tone which
     exists side by side with the "joy of Christian
     hope" in her poetry.

3    VENKATESAN, N. K. "Christina Georgina Rossetti.
     The Second Great Victorian Poetess," Educa-
     tional Review (Madras), XIX (May), 269-76.
         Although the essay is printed in several
     parts (See 1914.B1 for the remainder of the
     publication information), the entire essay is
     annotated here. Christina Rossetti is con-
     sidered as a "poetess of the Neo-Romantic
     Movement." Venkatesan discusses Christina
     Rossetti's childhood and early poems (1830-
     1847). "One wonders indeed how Miss Rossetti
     could, with her calmness of mind and serenity
     of temper, conceive such a horrible picture
     as that in her 'Will These Hands Ne'er be
     Clean?'" There is a tone of weariness and a

1913

(VENKATESAN, N. K.)
desire for rest seen in Christina Rossetti's
poetry after the broken engagement with
Collinson, seen especially in "How One Chose,"
"Repining," and "Sweet Death." Unlike Elizabeth Barrett Browning and George Eliot, who
"were anxious to establish woman's status as
distinct from men's," Christina Rossetti was
self-effacing and self-renouncing all of her
life. Venkatesan feels that "From House to
Home" transcends Tennyson's "Palace of Art."

1914 A   BOOKS - NONE

1914 B   SHORTER WRITINGS

1    VENKATESAN, N. K. "Christina Georgina Rossetti:
An Essay," Educational Review (Madras), XX
(April), 221-30; (August), 477-84; (Septem-
ber), 539-49.
A continuation of 1913.B3. For complete an-
notation, SEE 1913.B3.

2    _____. Christina Georgina Rossetti:  An Essay.
Madras:  Srinivasa Varadachari.  33 pp.
Reprint of 1913.B3 and 1914.B1.

1915 A   BOOKS

1    MARTIN, HELEN VIRGINIA. "Christina Rossetti:   A
Brief Survey of Her Life and Poetry." Masters
essay, Columbia University.  37 pp.
A description of Christina Rossetti's life
and family is followed by a consideration of
her poetry in general, which is viewed as the
outlet for her emotions. "A poet of beauty
and tenderness, Christina Rossetti is always

68

# CHRISTINA ROSSETTI: A REFERENCE GUIDE

(MARTIN, HELEN VIRGINIA)
purely feminine in her appeal. Her conclu-
sions are the results of intuition and emotion rather than the outcome of any process
of logical reasoning. There is, indeed,
little that is intentionally didactic in her
work. To be sure, there is always a moral
for those who require it, but it is rarely
forced upon the reader. He may take it for
what it is worth, or he may let it go; in
either case, the poetry is not impaired. To
try to interpret most of her poetry from an
ethical standpoint is the greatest mistake,
for the very origin and reason for its being
is against this quality."

## 1915 B   SHORTER WRITINGS

1    MASON, EUGENE. "Two Christian Poets: Christina
G. Rossetti and Paul Verlaine" in A Book of
Preferences in Literature. London:  John G.
Wilson; New York:  Dutton, pp. 115-37.
In the first part of the chapter Mason de-
scribes Christina Rossetti's life and volumes
of poetry. The two keynotes of her character
are "poetess and saint." Although Christina
Rossetti and Paul Verlaine were contemporar-
ies, "beyond their common faith and their
gift of devotional song, the two writers had
absolutely no meeting-ground. . . .
Verlaine's prototype is not Christina
Rossetti, but rather Francis Villon."

2    WAUGH, ARTHUR. "Christina Rossetti" in Reticence in Literature, and Other Papers. New
York:  E. P. Dutton, pp. 149-53.
Waugh feels that Christina Rossetti was not
really a part of the Pre-Raphaelite Brotherhood:  ". . . when she was thrown by fortune,

(WAUGH, ARTHUR.)
first of all into a general concerted movement
of men, and secondly into a movement con-
cerned with the very essentials of art, she
took, inevitably, the woman's way.  Slowly but
surely her personality . . . drifted towards
that sort of 'criticism of life' which was es-
sentially the very poetic method the Pre-
Raphaelites were banding together to
avoid. . . .  In short, the purpose and the
meaning of life become her insistent theme,
and the love of art, for its own sake, grows
inevitably less and less."

3    WILLIAMSON, CLAUDE C. H.  "A Few Lines on Christina Rossetti" in Writers of Three Centuries:
1789-1914.  Philadelphia:  George W. Jacobs,
pp. 270-72.
This short note praises Christina Rossetti's
simple, fresh style:  "To browse amongst her
poems is like wandering in the meadows in
May. . . .  Her lyrics have that desiderium,
that obstinate longing for something lost out
of life."


1916 A   BOOKS - NONE

1916 B   SHORTER WRITINGS

1    WATTS-DUNTON, THEODORE.  "IV.  Christina Georgina
Rossetti.  1830-1894" in Old Familiar Faces.
London:  Herbert Jenkins, pp. 177-206.
Reprint of 1895.B36 and 1896.B21.


1917 A   BOOKS - NONE

1917 B  SHORTER WRITINGS

  1    LAWSON, MALCOLM. "Music to Song of Christina
          Rossetti," N&Q, III (17 March), 214.
             In this note Lawson, who was at one time
          next-door neighbor to Dante Gabriel Rossetti,
          notes that he set "Song" ("When I am dead, my
          dearest") to music, published as "Hereafter."

  2    THOMPSON, A. HAMILTON. "Christina Rossetti" in
          The Cambridge History of English Literature.
          New York: Macmillan; Cambridge, England:
          Cambridge University Press, XIII, Part II,
          153-56.
             "Mystic though she was, her thought never
          found refuge in complicated or obscure lan-
          guage, but translated itself into words with
          the clearness and definiteness which were
          among the aims of the Pre-Raphaelite asso-
          ciates of her girlhood." She has the advan-
          tage over Elizabeth Browning in melodiousness
          of verse.

  3    WAINEWRIGHT, JOHN B. "Music to Song of Christina
          Rossetti," N&Q, III (10 March), 192.
             In this note Wainwright verifies that "Song"
          ("When I am dead, my dearest") was set to mu-
          sic by Malcolm Lawson and Alice Mary Smith.
          "J.S.S." states that the poem was set to mu-
          sic by S. Coleridge-Taylor. Both answers are
          responses to a query on p. 149 of the same
          volume of N&Q.

1918 A  BOOKS - NONE

1918 B  SHORTER WRITINGS

  1    HUDSON, WILLIAM HENRY. "Christina Rossetti" in
          A Short History of English Literature in the

(HUDSON, WILLIAM HENRY)
Nineteenth Century. London: G. Bell and
Sons, 143-45.
    After a brief sketch of her life and a list
of her major works, Hudson notes that Christina Rossetti's religious poetry is at times
"marred by quaintness and subtleties which
remind us of what is least admirable in the
writings of those seventeenth-century poets,
particularly Herbert and Crashaw, with whom
she has often been compared." Christina
Rossetti was superior to Elizabeth Barrett
Browning in "pure imagination" and in "intensity of poetic vision."

2   LUBBOCK, PERCY. "Christina Rossetti" in The
    English Poets: Selections With Critical In-
    troductions by Various Writers, ed. Thomas
    Humphry Ward. New York: Macmillan, V,
    286-90.
        Lubbock sees Christina Rossetti's poetry as
    an escape from "a code of duty unnaturally
    arid" into a "kind of beauty that was all
    earthly warmth and fragrance." Originality
    of meter and richness of style are seen in
    such poems as "Goblin Market" and "The
    Prince's Progress." Although "overhung with
    sterile shadows," her work manages to break
    out in "pure irresponsible music." The
    eleven poems which follow (pp. 290-300) in-
    clude "Dream Land," "A Birthday," "Up-Hill,"
    "Echo," and "Passing Away."

3   OLIVERO, FEDERICO. "Poeti Mistici: Richard
    Crashaw, Coventry Patmore, Christina Rossetti,
    Rabindranath Tagore" in Nuovi Saggi di Letter-
    atura Inglese. Torino: Libreria Editrice
    Internazionale, pp. 275-310.
        Christina Rossetti's poetry is discussed on
    pp. 289-95. Olivero notes the stress on the

(OLIVERO, FEDERICO)
    after-life, and discusses the religious poet-
    ry as the only way Christina Rossetti had of
    expressing her adoration for God. Her poetry
    is not only an escape from the pain and frus-
    tration of the realities of this life, but
    also an outlet for spiritual ardor. The
    "Monna Innominata" sonnets are a typical ex-
    ample of a factual recording of the nostalgia
    and anguish over an affection ignored, of a
    desolate love ending in silence and solitude.
    Such poems as "Goblin Market" create a pro-
    found emotion through vivid representation
    and richness of imagination. Her expression
    has the richness of Spenser and Keats. The
    short lyric is especially suited to her poetic
    nature, as it expresses the moment of spiri-
    tual epiphany rapidly and magnificently.

1919 A   BOOKS - NONE

1919 B   SHORTER WRITINGS

   1   MATHER, FRANK JEWETT, JR. "The Rossettis," Book-
           man (New York), XLIX (April), 139-47.
               This article gives a description of the mem-
           bers of the Rossetti household. Of Christina
           Rossetti he writes: "With the life-renouncing
           passion of Christina Rossetti I have the
           smallest sympathy; the exquisiteness of its
           results in poetry I cannot deny."

   2   OSMOND, PERCY H. "Christina Rossetti" in The
           Mystical Poets of the English Church. London:
           Society for Promoting Christian Knowledge,
           pp. 401-410.
               "Her fear lay at the root of her mysticism,
           for it proceeded from her intimate knowledge

1919

(OSMOND, PERCY H.)
of spiritual mysteries. It contained a deep
mistrust of self, but no misgiving about
God's goodness." Some of Christina
Rossetti's devotional prose and poetry reflect her earthly disappointments.

3    PARKER, ELIZABETH. "The Love Affairs of Christina Rossetti," University Magazine
(Montreal), XVIII (April), 246-55.
A description of Christina Rossetti's family and girlhood is followed by an account of
her engagement to Collinson and her life-long
love for Cayley.

4    WALKER, HUGH, and MRS. HUGH WALKER. Outlines of
Victorian Literature. Cambridge, England:
Cambridge University Press, pp. 82-83.
This is a brief (two paragraphs) discussion
of the influence of the Oxford Movement on
Christina Rossetti. Her refined simplicity
of style is contrasted with the gorgeous sen-
suousness of her brother's style.

1920 A   BOOKS

1    BOURNE, ANNA RUTH. "Christina Rossetti as Exponent of the English Pre-Raphaelite Movement."
Masters essay, Columbia University. 32 pp.
Bourne describes the Pre-Raphaelite protest
against the outworn traditions of the eighteenth century, and the characteristics of
Pre-Raphaelite painting and poetry. Bourne
views Christina Rossetti "not only as following their lead, but as guiding and inspiring
their tasks in the new idealism" (p. 13).
"Goblin Market" illustrates her delight in
sensuous beauty and richness of detail, and

1922

(BOURNE, ANNA RUTH)
"The Prince's Progress" is "bathed in the atmosphere of old romance" (p. 21). The faith
of Christina Rossetti was meditative in its
implicit unquestioning nature and its decided
ascetic bent.

1920 B  SHORTER WRITINGS

1      ELTON, OLIVER. "The Rossettis" in A Survey of
       English Literature, 1780-1880: In Four Vol-
       umes. London: Arnold; New York: Macmillan,
       IV, 22-30.
           "Her melancholy and austerity were inborn,
       and were increased by a certain tyrannical
       quality in her conscience." Elton categorizes
       Christina Rossetti's poetry into the fantas-
       tic, the religious, and the secular, and he
       discusses the best poems of each group. From
       the first group he selects "Goblin Market" as
       "a small masterpiece." "The Prince's Prog-
       ress" is "another glamour-story." Both poems
       are compared to Coleridge's "Ancient Mariner."
       In the second group are included the "Monna
       Innominata" sonnets. The third group, the
       secular and short songs, include "Song"
       ("When I am dead, my dearest"), "An End,"
       "Dream Land," and "A Birthday."

1922 A  BOOKS - NONE

1922 B  SHORTER WRITINGS

1      BEERBOHM, MAX. Cartoon in Rossetti and His
       Circle. London: Heinemann, 12.
           This caricature shows Dante Gabriel attempt-
       ing to persuade Christina Rossetti to dress
       less conservatively.

1922

2    SHUSTER, GEORGE N.  "Ruskin, Pater, and the
Pre-Raphaelites" in The Catholic Spirit in
Modern English Literature. New York: Macmillan, pp. 166-86. Christina Rossetti is
discussed on pp. 182-85.
    Shuster notes that her "life was a groping
realization of the Catholic instinct. It is
said that she was scrupulously careful not to
tread upon a scrap of paper in the street,
lest it should bear the Holy Name. Her writing might have been done upon her
knees. . . ."

3    WATSON, WILLIAM.  "To Christina Rossetti" in A
Hundred Poems. London: Hodder and Stoughton,
p. 179.
Revised version of 1905.B4.

1923 A  BOOKS

1    DE WILDE, JUSTINE FREDERIKA.  Christina Rossetti,
Poet and Woman. Nijkerk: C. C. Callenbach.
160 pp.
    This dissertation, done in Amsterdam, is
biographical and critical. Christina
Rossetti's letters reveal her as a sympathetic
and courageous woman with established opinions
of her own as well as a sense of humor.
Christina Rossetti and Dante Gabriel are compared as persons and as poets: Christina
Rossetti had greater spontaneity but Dante
Gabriel had greater craftsmanship, making
greater use of such devices as alliteration
and using more elaborate imagery in his poems.
Christina Rossetti's melancholy is reminiscent of the Middle Ages. She had a dualistic
concept of God and the universe. After defin-
ing mysticism several different ways De Wilde

# CHRISTINA ROSSETTI: A REFERENCE GUIDE

1923

(DE WILDE, JUSTINE FREDERIKA)
concludes that Christina Rossetti cannot
really be considered a mystical poet. The
chapter on Christina Rossetti's poetry closes
with a discussion of such technical merits as
clarity of form and variety of meter. The
final chapter summarizes contemporary opinion
and criticism of Christina Rossetti. A bibliography concludes the study.

2    MARSHALL, LOUISVILLE. "The Life of Christina
     Rossetti." Masters essay, Columbia University.
     77 pp.
         This account, based on Bell, Caine, Gosse,
     and Hueffer, utilizes letters written by
     Dante Gabriel and Christina Rossetti. Mar-
     shall relates Christina Rossetti's poetry to
     her personal experience, showing how she
     transformed the joys and sorrows of her own
     life into poems.

1923 B    SHORTER WRITINGS

1    BALD, MARJORY A. "Christina Rossetti: 1830-
     1894" in Woman-Writers of the Nineteenth Cen-
     tury. Cambridge, England: Cambridge Univer-
     sity Press, pp. 233-84.
         This chapter is divided into five parts:
     "I. Personal Experience Reflected in Her
     Poetry" describes the nearness of death in
     Christina Rossetti's life, due to poor health,
     and the renunciation which came with Chris-
     tina Rossetti's rejection of Collinson and
     Cayley. "II. Sources" lists Christina
     Rossetti's favorite authors--Bunyan, Shelley,
     Coleridge, and Keats. Dante was the strongest
     influence, but Christina Rossetti's chief
     source for all of her poems was her own life:
     "The most essential fact of her nature was her

77

(BALD, MARJORY A.)
singular independence of environment" (pp.
239-40).  The artistic merit and philosophy
of Christina Rossetti's work is compared with
that of Mrs. Browning.  "Christina's soul was
like a radiant texture, its colours flashing
and quivering as if some hidden life were
rippling through its folds.  Mrs. Browning's
soul was of the same colour, but in a paler
shade, and woven of plainer threads" (p. 251).
"III.  Symbol, Allegory, and Dream" deals
with the allegories of journeying in the
poems "The Dead City," "The Ballad of Boding,"
and "The Prince's Progress," and discusses
Christina Rossetti's use of symbol as Platon-
ic in its function as an approach to invisible
realities.  "IV.  Emotional Quality" notes a
recurring wistfulness and patient serenity
along with occasional escape into passion or
ecstasy.  "Monna Innominata" is "the only in-
stance of her yielding to imagination of the
might-have-been--love rendered without any
pang of renunciation" (p. 262).  "V.  General
Considerations" discusses the formal excel-
lences of Christina Rossetti's verse:  the
varied form of single lines, the use of the
shortened final line (as in "Passing Away"),
and the repetition of sounds without monotony
are illustrated and praised by Bald.  The conclusion is that Christina Rossetti "will be
remembered as a solitary, exquisite flower,
blooming for a season, fading, and casting no
seed" (p. 274).

2    BROERS, BERNARDA CONRADINA.  Mysticism in the
Neo-Romantics.  Amsterdam:  A. H. Kruyt, pp.
98-102.
Christina Rossetti is discussed as a religious mystic and ascetic.  Broers notes the

(BROERS, BERNARDA CONRADINA)
Pre-Raphaelite-like rapture of "A Birthday,"
and the sad remembrance of fiery passion of
"The Convent Threshold." She draws a parallel between "Despised and Rejected" and
Holman Hunt's famous picture "The Light of
the World."

3    SYMONS, ARTHUR. "The Rossettis" in Dramatis
Personae. Indianapolis: Bobbs-Merrill, pp.
118-31.
This essay describes Symon's friendship
with Christina Rossetti. "It always seems to
me that as she had read Leopardi and Baude-
laire, the thought of death had for her the
same fascination; only it is not the fascination of attraction, as with the one, nor re-
pulsion, as with the other, but of interest,
sad but scarcely unquiet interest in what the
dead are doing underground, in their memories,
if memory they have, of the world they have
left."

1924 A   BOOKS - NONE

1924 B   SHORTER WRITINGS

1    SYMONS, ARTHUR. "Christina Rossetti" in Studies
in Two Literatures, 2nd ed. London: Martin
Secker, pp. 135-49.
Reprint of 1897.B4.

1925 A   BOOKS - NONE

1925 B   SHORTER WRITINGS

1    MADELEVA M. "The Religious Poetry of the Nineteenth Century" in Chaucer's Nuns, and Other

1925

(MADELEVA, M.)
Essays. New York: D. Appleton, pp. 123-25.
In two paragraphs Madeleva notes the saint-
liness of Christina Rossetti's life; ". . .
her homesickness for heaven is near to hypo-
chondria, yet one cannot assail the patient
sweetness of it."


1926 A  BOOKS - NONE

1926 B  SHORTER WRITINGS

1    DE LA MARE, WALTER. "Christina Rossetti" in
     Essays by Diverse Hands, Being the Transac-
     tions of the Royal Society of Literature of
     the United Kingdom, ed. G. K. Chesterton.
     London: Milford, VI, 79-116.
     After a brief reiteration of Wordsworth's
     statement of the poetic process, he then de-
     scribes Christina Rossetti's love poems as
     being for the most part subjective, "intense-
     ly personal and emotional. . . . While she
     wrote even her most desperate and tragic
     poems, her mind was exalted, at a hazardous
     rest, and not only happy in the presence of
     the truth and reality she was striving to ex-
     press, but in the achievement of expressing
     them fully and truly" (p. 85). He views the
     serenity and self-control seen in her letters
     and in her life as stemming not from weakness,
     but from an unusual strength of mind and
     heart. Despite her secluded and quiet life,
     "that quiet mind was a reservoir of impas-
     sioned memories" (p. 105).

1928

## 1927 A  BOOKS

1   ELIOT, RUTH F.   "Elizabeth Barrett Browning and
Christina Rossetti:  A Comparison."  Masters
essay, Columbia University, 39 pp.
Elizabeth Browning "must be acknowledged to
have fallen far short of Christina Rossetti
in artistic execution and in poetic values. . . ."  Both poets, however, were "distinctly feminine" in their encounter with
life, and neither was a slave to the tradition of the period (p. 37).

## 1927 B   SHORTER WRITINGS

1   CLUTTON-BROCK, ARTHUR.   "Christina Rossetti" in
More Essays on Religion.  London:   Methuen,
pp. 11-23.
"She was religious with a meditative intensity of belief and devotion."  Clutton-Brock
compares Christina Rossetti with George
Herbert:   "Both are troubled by the insecurity
of their spiritual raptures."  He praises
Christina Rossetti's skillful use of rhythm:
"The metrical scheme itself is irregular so
that it may never become insistent and all ob-
vious cadences are avoided."

## 1928 A   BOOKS - NONE

## 1928 B   SHORTER WRITINGS

1   ANON.   "Memorabilia," N&Q, CLV (25 August), 127.
This brief article describes Christina
Rossetti's responses to queries concerning the
wording of the opening of the Prayer Book and
the historical Artemus Ward.

1928

2    CLUTTON-BROCK, ARTHUR. "Christina Rossetti" in
     More Essays on Religion. New York: Dutton,
     pp. 11-23.
     Reprint of 1927.B1.

3    COURTEN, MARIA LUISA GIARTOSIO de. "Chapter VII.
     Esperienze Poetiche e Sentimentali di
     Cristina" and "Chapter X. Gli Ultimi Anni di
     Cristina: Il Superstite" in I Rossetti:
     Storia di una Famiglia. Milano: Alpes, pp.
     181-214, 289-319.
        Chapter VII describes Christina Rossetti's
     life and her love for Collinson and Cayley.
     Chapter X analyzes such poems as "From House
     to Home," "Advent," and "Despised and Re-
     jected," and concludes with a consideration of
     Christina Rossetti's later years. Christina
     Rossetti had modern appeal because of the
     profound thoughtfulness, intensity of emo-
     tion, and sweetness of harmony characterizing
     her poetry.

4    THOMAS, EDWARD. "Christina Rossetti" in The Last
     Sheaf: Essays. London: Jonathan Cape, pp.
     65-70.
        Thomas considers Christina Rossetti to be
     the "greatest of the women among our poets."
     Her range is limited but her poetry has the
     enduring music of "a larch tree sighing in the
     wind."

1929 A  BOOKS

1    MARSHALL, DOROTHY VESTA. "The Poetry of Chris-
     tina Rossetti." Masters essay, University of
     Nebraska, 1929. 171 pp.
        This thesis is divided into three chapters,
     the first giving a biographical sketch of

(MARSHALL, DOROTHY VESTA)
Christina Rossetti, the second discussing major themes of her poetry such as nature, death, and love human and sublime. The third chapter discusses the metrics and poetic forms, such as the ballad and Christina Rossetti's bouts-rimés sonnets.

## 1929 B   SHORTER WRITINGS

1    FREND, GRACE GILCHRIST. "Great Victorians: Some Recollections of Tennyson, George Eliot and the Rossettis," Bookman (London), LXXVII (October), 9-11.
      Christina Rossetti is described as "shy and unassuming," and loving animals. Frend believes she was "the sweetest lyric singer of the Victorian era."

2    PETERSON, HOUSTON. "Christina Georgina Rossetti" in The Book of Sonnet Sequences, ed. Houston Peterson. London, New York, Toronto: Longmans, Green, pp. 291-92.
      Peterson gives a brief sketch of Christina Rossetti's life, and then reprints the fourteen "Monna Innominata" sonnets (pp. 293-300). "This sequence at once calls up the Sonnets from the Portuguese, a comparison which is not fair to Miss Rossetti as Monna Innominata is not on her highest level, although it does show clearly enough what Paul Elmere [sic] More considers her more 'feminine' spirit."

3    SERRA, BEATRICE. "Christina G. Rossetti," Nuova Antologia, CCCLXIV (1 July), 56-69.
      Christina Rossetti is described as a delicate, beautiful, austere woman who was aptly chosen to model for her brother's paintings. Her modest, retiring nature, her renunciation

1929

(SERRA, BEATRICE)
of the love of her two suitors, Collinson and
Cayley, and her sincerely religious nature
are reflected in her poetry. Christina
Rossetti's clear, lyrical poetic style is
praised, especially in such poems as "Dream
Land" and "Passing Away." The sadness of un-
fulfilled love comes through in much of
Christina Rossetti's poetry. Her work is
born of profound inspiration, augmented by
love and suffering.

1930 A    BOOKS

1    BIRKHEAD, EDITH. Christina Rossetti and Her
Poetry. London, Bombay, Sydney: Harrap.
127 pp.
This study is biographical and critical.
Although Christina Rossetti was little affected by the movements of her times, she was
awake to the realities of love and death.
Her melancholic nature was augmented by frequent illness. Birkhead believes that while
Christina Rossetti rejected James Collinson
on religious grounds, she refused Cayley because of "something inherent in her temperament, a partly unconscious recoil from in-
timate contact with any human being lest it
might violate a romantic ideal" (p. 41). As
Christina Rossetti grew older she began to
distrust the senses and therefore turned to
spiritual love. She found the practice of art
a solace "when the burden of herself became
intolerable" (p. 106). She was extremely sensitive to the sound of her verse as well as
her prose, earning thereby the admiration of
Swinburne and Walter De La Mare.

2    LINGO, JUNE INEZ.  "A Study of the Poetry of
     Christina Rossetti."  Masters essay, Univer-
     sity of Iowa.  68pp.
        This study is divided into three parts.
     The first considers the relations of Christina
     Rossetti to the Pre-Raphaelites, the second
     treats of her relationship to the Oxford Move-
     ment, and the last part notes the slight ef-
     fect of contemporaneous events upon Christina
     Rossetti's poetry.

3    SANDARS, MARY F.  The Life of Christina Rossetti.
     London:  Hutchinson.  291 pp.
        This biography, based largely on Bell and
     William Michael Rossetti, includes a number of
     Christina Rossetti's letters.  The account of
     Christina Rossetti's life contains many illus-
     trations, including a facsimile of her holo-
     graph Italian translation of "If a pig wore a
     wig," and descriptions of all of the major
     volumes of poetry and their critical recep-
     tions.

4    STUART, DOROTHY MARGARET.  Christina Rossetti
     (English Men of Letters Series).  London:
     Macmillan.  viii + 200 pp.
        The biographical part of the book is based
     on accounts of Christina Rossetti's life by
     her brother, William Michael Rossetti.  In the
     second half of the book, Stuart notes that
     Christina Rossetti follows the lead of Dante
     Gabriel in her ballads, and "in narratives and
     allegories she might set her feet where
     Tennyson had led the way; but in her lyrics
     she was what she had always been--passionately
     herself, and so she was to remain to the end"
     (p. 60).  Stuart finds "The Prince's Progress"
     inferior to "Goblin Market" because its moral
     is too clear.  Chapter VII is devoted to a

(STUART, DOROTHY MARGARET)
discussion of the sonnets, especially the
"Monna Innominata" sonnets. "She achieves in
these fourteen sonnets the perfect fusion of
emotion and language, the soul and the body of
poetry" (p. 132). The last chapter, "Epi-
logue," categorizes the poems as "Pre-
Raphaelite" or "non-Preraphaelite." "Goblin
Market" stands alone, outside of both cate-
gories, as does "The Prince's Progress."

## 1930 B  SHORTER WRITINGS

1    ANON. "Christina Rossetti," TLS (4 December),
1021-22.
The dissatisfaction marking Christina
Rossetti's later poetry of the 1880's is due
to the fact that Christina Rossetti was an
Italian forced to live in England, and she
could not adapt: "Her life was grounded on
an incongruity; from childhood up, the impressions she absorbed so delicately were impressions with which she was never perfectly
in tune."

2    ANON. "Rossetti Family in Bucks," N&Q, CLIX
(6 September), 176.
This inquiry into the Rossettis' residence
at Holmer Green is signed "S.V.B."

3    ANON. "To-day and Yesterday," Week-end Review,
II (13 December), 886.
Christina Rossetti is "at once Christian and
pagan, ascetic and sensuous, and that without
damaging contradiction." Although not as
great a poet as Robert Herrick, Christina
Rossetti has a "noble poetic nature." The reviewer cites as among Christina Rossetti's
masterpieces "The Convent Threshold" and "Amor

(ANON.)
Mundi." In comparing Christina Rossetti with
Elizabeth Barrett Browning the writer notes
that "Mrs. Browning is the poet the women of
her epoch would have wished her to be: Christina Rossetti is not."

4 DE LA MARE, WALTER JOHN. "Christina Rossetti"
in Christina Rossetti: Poems, Chosen by Wal-
ter de la Mare, With a Portrait Engraved on
Wood by R. Ashwin Maynard. Newton, Wales:
Gregnog Press, vii–xl.
Reprint of 1926.B1.

5 ELLIS, S. M. "A Hundred Years Ago: Christina
Rossetti (1830–1894)," Bookman (London),
LXXIX (December), 179–81.
Ellis gives a brief account of Christina
Rossetti's life and literary tastes: she en-
joyed Scott, Radcliffe, and Maturin, and began
writing poetry at the age of eleven. Ellis
describes Christina Rossetti's love for Collinson and Cayley, and includes "A hitherto
unpublished portrait of Christina Rossetti at
the age of sixteen" done by Dante Gabriel,
taken from Mary Sandars' biography, as well as
two other pictures of Christina Rossetti.

6 GREENE, KATHLEEN CONYNGHAM. "Christina Georgina
Rossetti: A Study and Some Comparisons,"
Cornhill Magazine, LXIX (December), 662–70.
Green compares Christina Rossetti's poetry
to that of contemporaneous poetesses, such as
Elizabeth Barrett Browning, Alice Meynell, and
Emily Dickinson. "A certain superficial like-
ness in their circumstances makes it tempting
to put her work beside that of Emily Dickinson, and then we miss in it the tang of bitterness that gives Emily Dickinson's verse its
particular flavour and quality." Christina

(GREENE, KATHLEEN CONYNGHAM)
Rossetti is criticized for having "always the
same mood" as well as for her casual "'habits
of composition'" and unconscious poetic technique; her poetry nevertheless displays an
"elusive, tremulous charm" and an artlessness
"that transcends all but the greatest art."

7    KENT, MURIEL. "Christina Rossetti: A Reconsideration," Contemporary Review, CXXXVIII
(December), 759-67.
Kent compares Christina Rossetti's passionate nature with that of Swinburne. "Both
were by nature ardent, passionate; but Swinburne's passion was to him like a fiery ban-
ner to be waved for an individual or a cause;
or the source of a verbal torrent to sweep all
Young Europe under the guidance of 'one red
star.' Passion in Christina Rossetti was the
strong still current of her inner life."

8    MOORE, VIRGINIA. "Letters and Comment: Christina Rossetti's Centennial," YR, XX (December), 428-32.
Moore believes that "from Sappho to Christina Rossetti no woman wrote poetry of the
first water." Christina Rossetti is a "woman
of Latin intensities" despite the fact that
she lived her entire life in London. The poetry is divided into love poems, philosophical
or religious poems, children's poems, and nature poems. Only a quarter of the poetry is
"irreproachably fine," but these poems have
been as yet read only superficially by the
public.

9    ROSSETTI, GEOFFREY W. "Christina Rossetti,"
Criterion, X (October), 95-117.
Geoffrey Rossetti, Christina Rossetti's
nephew, gives a brief sketch of her life, in-

(ROSSETTI, GEOFFREY W.)
cluding an excerpt from one of her letters to
Dante Gabriel in 1881. Of "Goblin Market" he
states: "Christina shows herself an accom-
plished master of metrical and rhythmical
subtleties. The apparent irregularity of the
poem is completely ordered and disciplined,
the variations of pace in the verse are fully
controlled" (p. 102). He discusses the quality of "fantasy" in other poems, such as "The
Prince's Progress," and includes selections
from some of Christina Rossetti's letters to
Cayley written in 1883. Christina Rossetti's
weaknesses are a too-narrow scope of experience (but this is also her strength, as with
Jane Austen) and an overly-stressed importance
of the after-life rather than the here and
now.

10  WAUGH, ARTHUR. "Christina Rossetti, December 5,
1830; December 5, 1930," Nineteenth Century,
CVIII (December), 787-98.
Christina Rossetti had "perfection of technique and sincerity of vision." The article
discusses her brief involvement in the Pre-
Raphaelite Movement, which effected "Goblin
Market" and "The Prince's Progress," which
are "deliberate exercises in poetic expression." Christina Rossetti's art and vision
"acclaim her the most perfect of all the
English women poets. . . ."

11  WOODS, MARGARET L. "Poets of the 'Eighties" in
The Eighteen-Eighties: Essays by Fellows of
the Royal Society of Literature, ed. Walter
de la Mare. Cambridge, England: Cambridge
University Press, pp. 7-8.
The paragraph devoted to Christina Rossetti
places her in a class by herself, for she

1930

(WOODS, MARGARET L.)
stood apart from contemporary literary movements, and her art was "not imitative but
highly individual. She had an ear which
guided her unerringly through the measures of
verse which must have seemed in the 'sixties
highly irregular."

12    WOOLF, VIRGINIA. "I Am Christina Rossetti," Nation and Athenaeum, XLVIII (6 December),
322-24.
This is a description of Christina
Rossetti's personality and poetry. "Indeed
so strange is the constitution of things, and
so great the miracle of poetry, that some of
the poems you wrote in your little back room
will be found adhering together in perfect
symmetry when the Albert Memorial is dust and
tinsel."

13    [ZABEL, MORTON D.] "Christina Rossetti and Emily
Dickinson," Poetry, XXXVII (October), 213-16.
"Between these two women no comparison need
be forced. They lived in different worlds but
each found in isolation the fulfilment [sic]
of high lyric impulse. . . . Each knew the
inexorable laws of personal integrity, and, by
obeying them, gained her spiritual freedom and
her immortality." The article is signed
"M.D.Z."

1931 A   BOOKS

1    SHOVE, FREDEGOND. Christina Rossetti: A Study.
Cambridge, England: Cambridge University
Press. xvi + 120 pp.
The book is divided into three sections, the
first biographical, the second dealing with

(SHOVE, FREDEGOND)
Christina Rossetti's poetry, and the third
with her prose. A concluding chapter places
Christina Rossetti in the context of her own
times. The biographical account gives no
clue as to the cause of the love poems of
1857-1858 except to say that Christina
Rossetti pined long after the close of her
first love affair, which occurred in the
spring of 1850 (p. 13). The chapter on Christina Rossetti's poetry describes and praises
"Goblin Market," "The Prince's Progress," and
"Maiden Song." Shove believes that the
"Monna Innominata" sonnets must be read with
biographical references to Christina
Rossetti's struggle between inclination and
duty. These sonnets are not among Christina
Rossetti's best purely lyrical work (p. 48).
The children's poems reflect "the enchantment
of life itself" (p. 55). At the heart of
Christina Rossetti's genius is her ability to
observe God in the earth around her. Her Pre-
Raphaelite vividness and realistic, detailed
portraits are often overridden by spiritual
concerns, especially by her love of God.
Shove finds the prose to be inferior to the
poetry; the prose books "live mainly on account of the wonderful uprushing of lyrical
poetry that is in them" (p. 104). Chapter IV,
"Christina Rossetti in the Pattern of Her
Time," contrasts Christina Rossetti with some
of her contemporaries, such as Dante Gabriel
Rossetti and Elizabeth Barrett Browning.

2    STUART, DOROTHY MARGARET. Christina Rossetti
(English Association Pamphlet No. 78). Lon-
don: Oxford. 18 pp.
Stuart notes that "though Gosse called
Christina Rossetti the High Priestess of Pre-

1931

(STUART, DOROTHY MARGARET)
Raphaelitism, and though she sympathized with
the activities and--up to a certain point--
shared the views and endorsed the principles
of her brother and his friends, her essential
aloofness was broken by these things hardly
at all" (p. 4). Stuart describes Christina
Rossetti's life as "uneventful," and speaks
of her two manners, "the colourful and the
quiet" (p. 11). The two main sources of her
poetic inspiration were religious or spiritual love and secular or earthly love, the latter centering around Collinson and Cayley.
Stuart notes Christina Rossetti's "straitness"
(p. 15) in her orthodox views of religion.
In her conclusion Stuart places Christina
Rossetti above Elizabeth Barrett Browning because of "those counterpoised virtues of
splendour and austerity, asceticism and passion, candour and restraint which she [Chris-
tina] possessed in a measure so ample and
exercised in a manner so great" (p. 18).

3    THOMAS, ELEANOR WALTER. Christina Georgina
     Rossetti. New York: Columbia University
     Press. viii + 229 pp.
     Originally a dissertation, this biography is
based on accounts by Bell and William Michael
Rossetti, supplemented with Christina
Rossetti's letters. Thomas related Christina
Rossetti's poetry to the milieu in which she
lived. The Victorian world of art is briefly
sketched at the opening of the book, followed
by the biographical portion of the book (pp.
8-119). The remainder of the book offers a
categorization and explanation of the various
themes and images of Christina Rossetti's poetry. The poems are divided into those dealing with "the unapparent world" (vision, alle-

1931

(THOMAS, ELEANOR WALTER)
gory, ghosts, and goblins); poems of the material world and of the personal life; children's poems and short stories; and devotional poetry. In the chapter entitled "The Unapparent World" Thomas notes that the lus-
ciousness of forbidden fruit, as presented in
"Goblin Market," is summed up in Emily Dickinson's quatrain, "'Forbidden fruit a flavor
has / That lawful orchards mocks; / How lus-
cious lies the pea within / The pod that Duty
locks'" (p. 156). A bibliography of works by
and about Christina Rossetti (pp. 213-22) concludes the study.

4    WALTERS, HILDRED A. "A Comparison of Christina
Rossetti and Emily Dickinson as Poets of the
Inner Life." Masters essay, University of
Colorado. 79 pp.
Walters compares the religious differences,
secluded life, and emphasis on the inner self
of the two poetesses. Emily Dickinson re-
volted from the established religion while
Christina Rossetti remained a devout Anglican
all of her life, repressing her feelings of
love in order to be more devoted to Christ.
Both poets desired peace and escape from the
self, as expressed in their poetry, but Christina Rossetti was more explicit in her use of
imagery than was Emily Dickinson. Walters
concludes that the differences in the two
poets far outweigh their similarities.

1931 B   SHORTER WRITINGS

1    ANON. "Christina Rossetti," Contemporary Review,
CXXXIX (April), 540-42.
"Christina Rossetti belongs to the long line
of mystics, and inasmuch as she was a poet she

93

1931

(ANON.)
inevitably sings songs that look on the earth
as a place of passage.  But she had also the
faith of a mystic and that gives her poems,
apart altogether from their technical excellence and their amazing and almost biblical
restraint in the use of adjectives, an immor-
tal quality."  The article is signed
"J.E.G. de M."

2    ANON. . Review of Stuart's Christina Rossetti,
     English Review, LII (February), 255-56.
        Christina Rossetti is described as a
     "strict puritan" whose "creed suggested that
     the world and all its people were essentially
     evil. . . .  Her verse was morbid and grim be-
     fore she met with disappointments in
     love. . . ."  Nevertheless, "in her particular
     vein Christina has not been surpassed and she
     was fortunate in her lifetime in securing
     praise worth having. . . ."

3    ANON.  Review of Stuart's Christina Rossetti,
     Quarterly Review, CCLVI (April), 411.
        After one hundred years Christina Rossetti's
     influence is stronger than ever on "the
     thoughtful and religious-minded public. . . .
     It may be that Christina's sad grey spirit of
     contemplation helps these times which so re-
     cently were passing through fiery and angry
     ordeals.  The joy of her muse was certainly
     subdued, and always an element of wistfulness
     softened her sedate playfulness.  It is a pity
     that her environment or upbringing kept her
     imagination within cloistered limits, for it
     was a lovely and Blake-like dream that she had
     of the wave of yellow light sweeping at dawn
     from the trees of Regent's Park, as the cap-
     tive canaries of London there nightly assem-
     bled winged their ways back to their cages."

4    MORSE, B. J.  "Some Notes on Christina Rossetti
        and Italy," Anglia, LV, 101–5.
            Morse notes that Christina Rossetti is not
        so insular as is commonly believed.  He also
        points out that she did not write a single
        impassioned poem on England.

5    OBERTELLO, ALFREDO.  "Cristina Rossetti, nel
        Centenario della Sua Nascita," Rassegna
        Italiana, XIV (January), 16–30.
            This article is divided into three sections:
        Christina Rossetti's life, her English poems,
        and her Italian peoms.  Obertello praises
        "Goblin Market" and "Maiden Song" for their
        grace and simplicity, and he compares Chris-
        tina Rossetti's religious poetry with that of
        Vaughan, Crashaw, and Herbert.  "Italia, io Ti
        Saluto" and "Iddio c'illumini" are among her
        best Italian poems.  Obertello concludes that
        Christina Rossetti is great as an English and
        an Italian poetess.

6    REILLY, JOSEPH J.  "Christina Rossetti," America:
        A Catholic Review of the Week, XLIV (14 Febru-
        ary), 460–61.
            Reilly describes Christina Rossetti as an
        "imaginative, sensitive, restrainedly but
        deeply passionate" poet.  After categorizing
        her poetry into the light and fantastic, the
        devotional, and the secular, Reilly quotes
        from the best poems in each category.

7    WHITNEY, ELIZABETH BOYCE.  "The Oxford Movement
        and Its Influence on English Poetry."  Masters
        essay, University of Oklahoma, pp. 58–60.
            In Chapter IV, "Medievalism," Whitney notes
        that Christina Rossetti moved in the "medieval
        woman's sphere of loving and grieving."
        Christina Rossetti "deserves a place beside

1931

(WHITNEY, ELIZABETH BOYCE)
Keble and Newman if for no other reason than
that she so closely paralleled their religious poems. Her faith was of that calm,
deep virile kind like theirs. And like them
she put very little stress upon the imaginative, the visual imagery and symbolism of the
past, but was decidedly its spiritual interpreter."

1932 A   BOOKS

1    TEASDALE, SARA. "Christina Rossetti."
Unpublished, unfinished biography of Christina Rossetti, under the jurisdiction of
Margaret Conklin, Literary Executor of the
Estate of Sara Teasdale. Conklin has given
permission to an English professor to publish
the manuscript in his forthcoming book, and it
is therefore not available for scholars to see
at this time. Probably one reason that Sara
Teasdale's biography is entered in most of the
major Victorian bibliographies as being published in 1932 is that it received advance
publicity from Macmillan, which was eager to
publish it, and in such reviews as that by
Morris Schappes of the biographies of Dorothy
Stuart and Eleanor Thomas (See 1932.B6) where
Schappes mentions another biography "now in
preparation" which "will soon be published by
Miss Sara Teasdale." Margaret Haley Carpenter, in her recent biography of Sara Teasdale
(New York: Schulte, 1960), describes the effort which Sara Teasdale put into her manuscript. "While Sara was in the midst of writing the book, several other biographies of the
English poet were published, as she mentioned
in her Prefatory Note, and she decided that it

(TEASDALE, SARA)
would be advisable for her to return to England to speak personally with Miss Rossetti's
two nieces and to acquire some fresh material"
(p. 314). However, in England she contracted
pneumonia, which, along with a weak heart,
caused her death in January of 1933. After
quoting from some of the best parts of the
manuscript, Carpenter concludes, "The less
than one hundred pages that Sara left of her
manuscript are enough to convince the reader
that the unfinished book was a distinct loss
to literature" (p. 313). Teasdale's fairly
extensive notes contain several interesting
observations: "'C. R.'s sense of music in
English verse is infinitely more acute than
E. B. B.'s. Note the flat, ugly singsong of
even such a nobly conceived poem as "Cowper's
Grave" in comparison with any poem by C. R.
Even her least verses have a sense of the
necessity of variety in the beat'" (p. 310).
Later Teasdale notes: "'She carved her life
carefully as she might have carved a gem. A
person who knew Christina, but who insists on
remaining nameless, told me that the poet
loved deeply a man who was married--a facet of
her emotion that has never caught the light--
but that she would not have his love at the
cost of sorrow to his wife'" (p. 313).

1932 B   SHORTER WRITINGS

1    HUNT, VIOLET.  The Wife of Rossetti:  Her Life
     and Death.  London:  John Lane; New York:
     Dutton, pp. xiii, 296.
        Violet Hunt does not like Christina
     Rossetti, who did not particularly like
     Elizabeth Siddal.  Although Hunt notes that
     Christina Rossetti had more passion in her

(HUNT, VIOLET)
little finger than Lizzie had in her "whole
white body," she blames Christina Rossetti in
part for Lizzie's end: "Here was a chance
for nun-like charity. Her neglect of this
hapless sister in Christ is a stain on the
effulgence of a great and noble woman, deeper
far than the projected over-stepping of the
convent threshold . . . for which she did
self-imposed penance for the rest of her
life." Hunt also reveals Christina
Rossetti's "well kept" secret that in 1857
Christina Rossetti's sister Maria prevented
Christina Rossetti from eloping with James
Collinson (a married man) by lying across the
front door mat every night for a week.

2    KLENK, HANS. "D. Die Dichtergestalten. a)
Christina Rossetti. 1830-1894" in Nach-
wirkungen Dante Gabriel Rossettis. Unter-
suchungen an Werken von Christina Rossetti,
Coventry Patmore, Philip Bourke Marston,
Theodore Watts-Dunton, Arthur W. E.
O'Shaughnessy, Ernest Dowson, John Davidson.
Berlin: Bachmann, pp. 42-44.
Klenk expresses admiration for the simple
yet noble diction of Christina Rossetti's
poems. He also compares her poems with those
of her brother.

3    MACKENZIE, MARGARET. "Fettered Christina
Rossetti," Thought, VII (June), 32-43.
This centennial essay on Christina Rossetti
is divided into four parts, the first describing her life, the second discussing her religious outlook, Part III dealing with the
Italian influences on Christina Rossetti's poetry, and lastly a conclusion. Mackenzie
feels that Christina Rossetti should have been

1932

(MACKENZIE,,MARGARET)
a Catholic, although her fundamental religion
was Evangelical in spirit if not in creed.
"Fate had robbed her of her Catholic inheri-
tance and imprisoned her in the falsity of
the English Church," which explains Christina
Rossetti's dislike of Mariolatry.

4    MORSE-BOYCOTT, DESMOND. "Christina Rossetti,
     1830-1894" in Lead, Kindly Light: Studies of
     the Saints and Heroes of the Oxford Movement.
     London: The Centenary Press, pp. 121-27.
         This chapter gives a brief description of
     Christina Rossetti's life and volumes of po-
     etry, but does not mention any connection
     with the Oxford Movement, except that she ad-
     mired "the Father of Ritualism," Dr. Little-
     dale.

5    REILLY, JOSEPH J. "Christina Rossetti: Poet of
     Renunciation" in Dear Prue's Husband and Other
     People. New York: Macmillan, pp. 144-61.
         This chapter gives a biographical sketch,
     followed by a discussion of the poems. "In
     Christina Rossetti's life poetry played a
     highly important part. It provided an outlet
     for the emotions and spiritual yearnings of
     this sensitive, delicately conscienced woman
     whose ardent nature had made its great renun-
     ciation and crowned its high desires not with
     bridal lilies but with thorns" (p. 146).

6    SCHAPPES, MORRIS U. Review of Stuart's Christina
     Rossetti, Symposium, III (January), 123-28.
         In discussing Christina Rossetti's poetry,
     Schappes writes: "The woman who denied two
     lovers because of religious differences and
     who relinquished the joy of playing checkers
     because she was sinfully eager to win applied

(SCHAPPES, MORRIS U.)
that negation to her poetry and produced what
is probably the least sensuous style of any
nineteenth-century poet. . . . As a result
Christina Rossetti has little direct notation
of quivering sensuous experience, and, therefore, an astonishingly small number of
images." Schappes finds Christina Rossetti's
imagination "quite conventional, tepid," as
in "Up-Hill." Only a few poems, such as
"Goblin Market," "Noble Sisters," and "The
Convent Threshold," deserve consideration.

7    TUELL, ANNE KIMBALL. "Christina Rossetti" in A
Victorian at Bay. Boston: Marshall Jones,
pp. 49-60.
This is an evaluation of the spirit of
Christina Rossetti's poetry. "It is, however,
the stark intensity of Christina's best which
is its reality. Her authentic word is no
casual utterance or 'solitary recreation.'
It tells in shuddering honesty of a soul's
dark night sustained through the shuttered
years without persuasion of the heavenly vision of which at least the mirage is usually
held necessary for support. It has its
flashes of assault, seeks at moments 'to lay
violent hands on heaven's high treasury.'
But the deepest confession is of vibrant
quietude, like the flaming patience of the
souls in Dante's Purgatorio careful not to
get outside their most precious fire" (pp.
54-55).

8    WALLER, R. D. "Chapter Eight. Christina" in
The Rossetti Family, 1824-1854. Manchester:
Manchester University Press, pp. 217-42.
Waller describes what he considers to be
Christina Rossetti's "enigmatic" personality.

(WALLER, R. D.)
"It is impossible to understand Christina
Rossetti at all unless one begins by realis-
ing that she was not in middle age 'too late
for joy,' but was hardly born to it at
all. . . . Her nature was too tentative ever
to impose terms on the world around; hence
her fear of it, and her renunciation" (pp.
219-20). He analyzes Maude as reflective of
Christina Rossetti's "occasional liveliness"
as well as her "intellectual pride and aloofness" (p. 222). Waller ascribes the gloom and
fearful questioning of her love poems of the
fifties to her broken engagement to Collinson;
her "instinct for retirement" is the prominent
feature of her "beautiful and unobtrusive personality" (p. 242).

9    WOOLF, VIRGINIA. "I Am Christina Rossetti" in
     Second Common Reader. New York: Harcourt,
     Brace, pp. 257-65.
     Reprint of 1930.B12.


1933 A   BOOKS

1    BUCK, ELIZABETH FLEMING. "A Comparison of the
     Poetry of Christina Rossetti and Emily Dickin-
     son." Masters essay, University of Arizona.
     98 pp.
       The parallels are in their secluded lives,
     introspective natures, and unhappy love af-
     fairs. The poetry of both shows dominant
     themes of nature, religion, death, love, and
     immortality, but the treatment of these themes
     is vastly different. Christina Rossetti is
     more traditional in her treatment of religious
     themes and images, but Emily Dickinson treats
     religion with irreverent mischief and scorns
     conventional ideas.

1933

2    DUBSLAFF, FRIEDRICH.  Die Sprachform der Lyrik
     Christina Rossettis (Studien zur Englischen
     Philologie, No. 77).  Halle:  Max Niemeyer.
     vi + 94 pp.
         This was a dissertation written at
     Göttingen in 1933.  Dubslaff divides the fig-
     urative language of Christina Rossetti's po-
     etry into four categories:  similes, personi-
     fications, metaphorical elements, and symbols.
     He also discusses Christina Rossetti's favor-
     ite stylistic devices, such as biblical lan-
     guage, rhetorical questions, and repetition
     of sounds.  Dubslaff concludes that Christina
     Rossetti's mastery of various forms and de-
     vices was surprisingly great.

3    STEWART, BELLA CRAIG.  "Christina Rossetti:  A
     Singer of Death."  Masters essay, George Pea-
     body College.  152 pp.
         This study analyzes the contents of the 470
     poems dealing with death that are found in
     The Poetical Works.  Stewart's conclusion is
     that Christina Rossetti was a fatalist and
     was obsessed with the thought of death.  "She
     saw the inevitableness of death in everything.
     In a perfect fragrant rose she saw its ulti-
     mate withering; in the damask-cheek peach, its
     final decay; in spring she visualized winter,
     and in youth she saw death.  In the aftermath
     of death she saw peace and she desired it
     fiercely" (p. 149).

1933 B   SHORTER WRITINGS

1    BARDI, PIETRO.  "Eta Vittoriana:  Cristina Geor-
     gina Rossetti" in Storia della Letturatura
     Inglese.  Bari:  Gius, Laterza and Figli, pp.
     184-85.
         In the paragraph devoted to Christina
     Rossetti, Bardi praises her profound religious

1933

(BARDI, PIETRO)
   faith, simple, delicate style, and her sincerity. Her main volumes of poetry are listed.

2  EVANS, B. IFOR. "The Sources of Christina
   Rossetti's 'Goblin market,'" Modern Language
   Review, XXVIII (April), 156-65.
      Evans analyzes "Goblin Market" as derived
   from Arabian Nights, Keightley's Fairy Myth-
   ology, and Hone's Every-Day Book.

3  _____. "Christina Georgina Rossetti" in English
   Poetry in the Later Nineteenth Century. London: Methuen, pp. 65-80.
      Following a sketch of Christina Rossetti's
   life and poetry, Evans summarizes the ideas
   presented in 1933.B2. After analyzing the
   nature imagery in some of the poems from her
   earlier volumes and some of the devotional
   poems from her later volumes, he concludes
   that few writers "united so fully the two
   main and usually distinct movements of the
   period--the poetry with Pre-Raphaelite décor
   and the poetry of religious sensibility."

4  GREBANIER, FRANCES. [FRANCES WINWAR.] "Christina" in Poor Splendid Wings: The Rossettis
   and Their Circle. Boston: Little, Brown,
   pp. 22-30.
      The chapter describes Christina Rossetti's
   childhood, her engagement with Collinson, and
   the illness she suffered when the engagement
   was broken. Christina Rossetti's love for
   Collinson lived on long after it was buried,
   even after she had met and become interested
   in Charles Cayley: "Those Italian love poems
   were addressed to Cayley: the yearning often
   was for Collinson" (p. 312). Christina
   Rossetti is mentioned in passing throughout
   the book.

1933

5     SHIPTON, IRENE A. M.   "Christina Rossetti:   The
          Poetess of the Oxford Movement," Church Quar-
          terly Review, CXVI (July), 219-29.
             Shipton gives an account of Christina
          Rossetti's life, based on William's "Memoir."
          "The motive-power of Christina's life was re-
          ligion, and in the Oxford Movement she found
          her spiritual home." She kept the precepts of
          the Church strictly, and was "a Tractarian in
          the best sense of the word." Her devotional
          prose and poetry show "a familiar acquaint-
          ance with the minor as well as the major fes-
          tivals of the Church's Year."

6     THOMPSON, A. HAMILTON.   "Christina Rossetti" in
          The Cambridge History of English Literature.
          New York:  Macmillan; Cambridge, England:
          Cambridge University Press, XIII, Part II,
          153-56.
          Reprint of 1917.B2.


1934 A   BOOKS

1     SMITH, ETHEL MAY.   "Christina Rossetti and Her
          Critics."  Masters essay, Louisiana State
          University.  135 pp.
             This is a collection of critical estimates
          of a majority of Christina Rossetti's most
          prominent critics, preceded by a short sketch
          of her life.

1934 B   SHORTER WRITINGS

1     CUNLIFFE, JOHN W.   "Mid-Victorian Poets.   Chris-
          tina Rossetti (1830-1894)" in Leaders of the
          Victorian Revolution.  New York:  D. Appleton-
          Century, pp. 239-40.
             Cunliffe ranks Christina Rossetti as the
          greatest of all the women poets of the nine-

1934

(CUNLIFFE, JOHN W.)
teenth century. He gives a brief description
of her life, concluding with a quotation from
"Up-Hill."

2    HEARN, LAFCADIO. "The Minor Singers: Miss
Rossetti" in Complete Lectures: A History of
English Literature, One-volume edition.
Tokyo: Hokuseido, pp. 749-51.
   Hearn praises Christina Rossetti as the best
of the minor English poets, far above Elizabeth Browning, for her variety of subject and
the perfect form of her work: "perfect with
that severe beauty, born of perfect self-
control, which we should expect to find in
the work of a man rather [than] in that of a
woman."

3    MOORE, VIRGINIA. "III. Christina Rossetti" in
Distinguished Women Writers. New York: E. P.
Dutton, pp. 45-58.
   "Just as she liked to be horrified, she
liked to be destitute and forlorn. At seven-
teen, before she had had a love, she was la-
menting his loss." Moore believes that although Christina Rossetti's work has been
read only superficially, it can rightfully
claim "high poetic distinction" because of
"her ability to saturate a poem with values
beyond temporary considerations, so that one
forgets, as one reads, all other values."

4    GREBANIER, FRANCES. [FRANCES WINWAR.] "Christina" in Poor Splendid Wings: The Rossettis
and Their Circle. London: Hurst and
Blackett, pp. 22-30.
Reprint of 1933.B4.

# CHRISTINA ROSSETTI: A REFERENCE GUIDE

1936

<u>1936 A   BOOKS - NONE</u>

<u>1936 B   SHORTER WRITINGS</u>

1    BOYLE, SIR EDWARD. "Christina Rossetti" in
     <u>Biographical Essays, 1790-1890</u>. London: Ox-
     ford University Press, pp. 193-203.
         This essay describes the members of the
     Rossetti family and gives an account of Chris-
     tina's life. Boyle concludes that "within
     the limits which she deliberately set herself
     few poets, certainly no woman poet, has writ-
     ten in our tongue with the musical and metri-
     cal power or with the depth and sensitiveness
     of feeling which were hers."

2    GREEN, ZAIDEE EUDORA. "A Saint by Chance,"
     <u>English Review</u>, LXII (March), 330-37.
         Green feels that the woman who as a "young
     child was imperious, wilful, and self-centred"
     became a self-made martyr in her two love af-
     fairs. Christina Rossetti "was romantically
     in love with her woes, and, most important of
     all, hers was an intensely passionate nature,
     capable, if she had not chosen to play the
     role of saint, of arousing a less fickle na-
     ture than Collinson's, an even more remote
     nature than Cayley's."

3    UNTERMEYER, LOUIS. "Christina Rossetti" in <u>Mod-
     ern British Poetry: A Critical Anthology</u>,
     4th Revised Edition. New York: Harcourt,
     Brace, pp. 19-24.
         Following the brief biographical sketch is
     the remark that in all of Christina Rossetti's
     volumes of verse, "first and fifth-rate mingle
     uncritically, inextricably." Of Christina
     Rossetti's <u>Verses</u> (1893) Untermeyer notes,
     "Buried among the four hundred and fifty devo-

(UNTERMEYER, LOUIS)
    tional pieces given to the Society for Promot-
    ing Christian Knowledge, are some of the bit-
    terest but most authentic verse she ever
    wrote." The selections from Christina
    Rossetti's work (pp. 24-34) include "The
    Bourne," "From House to Home," "A Birthday,"
    "Dream Land," "Echo," "Passing Away," and
    "Song" ("When I am dead, my dearest").


1937 A    BOOKS - NONE

1937 B    SHORTER WRITINGS

1    HOPKINS, GERARD MANLEY. "A Voice from the World.
        Fragments of 'An Answer to Miss Rossetti's
        Convent Threshold'" in The Notebooks and
        Papers of Gerard Manley Hopkins, Edited with
        Notes and a Preface by Humphry House. London
        and New York: Oxford University Press, pp.
        16-21.
            This lengthy poem provides a response to
        the departure heavenward of the speaker in
        "The Convent Threshold"; Hopkins writes,

            Your comfort is as sharp as swords;
            And I cry out for wounded love.
            And you are gone so heavenly far
            You hear nor care of love and pain.

2    TROXELL, JANET CAMP. "IX. Christina Rossetti
        and The Prince's Progress" and "X. Christina
        Rossetti and Her Letters" in Three Rossettis:
        Unpublished Letters to and from Dante Gabriel,
        Christina, William. Cambridge, Mass.:
        Harvard University Press, pp. 138-80.
            The letters of Chapter IX show the problems
        encountered by Christina Rossetti as she

1937

(TROXELL, JANET CAMP)
prepared a volume for Macmillan to publish.
The letters in Chapter X reveal Christina
Rossetti's admiration for Dante Gabriel as
well as her modest, deferential nature.


1938 A   BOOKS - NONE

1938 B   SHORTER WRITINGS

1     RALEIGH, WALTER.  "Christina Rossetti" in Cham-
bers's Cyclopaedia of English Literature.
London:  W. and R. Chambers, III, 646-48.
Reprint of 1904.B9.


1939 A   BOOKS

1     HIGHLEY, MONA PATROCINIO.  "Elizabeth Barrett
Browning and Christina Georgina Rossetti:
A Comparative Study."  Masters essay,
University of Texas.  vi + 121 pp.
Highley contrasts the lives, poetic theo-
ries, and major poetic themes of these two
poets.  She concludes:  "Of the two women,
Mrs. Browning is undoubtedly the outright
moralist and minor poet; Christina, the more
spontaneous singer, hardly a moralist, and
certainly a great poet" (p. 115).

1939 B   SHORTER WRITINGS - NONE


1940 A   BOOKS - NONE

1940 B   SHORTER WRITINGS

1     LUCAS, F. L.  "Christina Rossetti" in Ten Victorian Poets.  Cambridge, England:  Cambridge

(LUCAS, F. L.)
  University Press, 115-37.
    Lucas notes that Christina Rossetti never
  met her gladiator. After a description of
  her life and poems, Lucas states: "This
  Mariana of Albany Street was born to have
  been one of the great lovers of history."
  Christina Rossetti is medieval in her morbid
  contemplation of death and her obsession with
  the grave, as well as in her passionate and
  childlike faith.


1942 A  BOOKS - NONE

1942 B  SHORTER WRITINGS

  1    BELLOC, ELIZABETH. "Christina Rossetti," Catho-
         lic World, CLV (September), 674-78.
           Dante Gabriel knew how great Christina
         Rossetti was: "greater than he." Christina
         was tainted by the "cult of sickliness" char-
         acteristic of the women of her age; "even as
         Euripides loved hate, so did Christina
         Rossetti love grief, and found its sad face
         fair."

  2    BROWN, E. K. "Christina Rossetti" in Victorian
         Poetry. New York: Ronald Press, p. 528.
           A chronological table is followed by a brief
         description of Christina Rossetti's poetry.
         "Less than almost any other Victorian poet
         does she 'date.'" Against much of her poetry
         "the charge of colorlessness and thinness can
         properly be urged; such defects were inevi-
         table in the work of a poet who was produc-
         tive, incapable of self-criticism and devoted
         to an ideal of economical, unemphatic, ex-
         quisite simplicity." Pages 528-43 reprint

1942

(BROWN. E. K.)
thirty-two of her poems, including all four-
teen of the "Monna Innominata" sonnets,
"Dream Land," "Up-Hill," "A Birthday,"
"Echo," "Amor Mundi," "Goblin Market," "A
Dirge," and "The Lowest Place."

3    SITWELL, EDITH. "Christina Rossetti: 1830-1894"
in English Women. London: William Collins,
pp. 41-43.
Edith Sitwell notes that the church weighed
too heavily on Christina Rossetti's poetry.
"Goblin Market, perhaps the most perfect poem
written by a woman in the English language,
this is the work of her nature,--not the slow,
dim, clay-cold verses of her religious life."
A brief sketch of Christina Rossetti's life
follows.

1947 A   BOOKS - NONE

1947 B   SHORTER WRITINGS

1    BUYS, R. VAN BRAKELL. "Christina Rossetti" in
Drie Dichteressen uit het Victoriaanse
Tijdperk. Christina Rossetti, Emily Brontë,
Elizabeth Barrett Browning, Hoogtepunten der
Engelse Cultuur, No. 3. Amsterdam: H. J. W.
Becht, pp. 7-50.
The twenty poems (pp. 40-50), including
"Amor Mundi," "Up-Hill," "Life and Death,"
"Rest," "Remember," and nine of the "Monna
Innominata" sonnets, are preceded by a crit-
ical introduction. After an account of her
life, Buys relates Christina Rossetti's poor
health to her dwelling on death in much of her
poetry, such as "Song" ("When I am dead, my
dearest"), "Remember," and "Sleeping at Last."

(BUYS, R. VAN BRAKELL)
   Christina Rossetti's poetry is compared to
   that of Shelley and Keats for its clarity of
   style and lyrical qualities.  Buys praises
   "Goblin Market" as one of Christina Rossetti's
   greatest works, and compares it to Coleridge's
   "Ancient Mariner" in its use of allegory.
   Christina Rossetti's poetry reflects her
   sense of isolation and grief, as well as her
   love of God.  The essay closes with the quotation of "Passing Away."

2   MEYNELL, ALICE.  "Christina Rossetti" in Prose
     and Poetry.  London:  Jonathan Cape, pp.
     145-48.
        This is a brief description of Christina
     Rossetti's poetry.  "An easy world is hers,
     and not only easy but beautiful."  Meynell
     thinks "The Convent Threshold" contains "more
     passion than in any other poem written by a
     woman."


1948 A   BOOKS - NONE

1948 B   SHORTER WRITINGS

1   LUCAS, F. L.  "Christina Rossetti" in Ten Vic-
     torian Poets, 3rd ed.  Cambridge, England:
     Cambridge University Press, pp. 115-37.
     Reprint of 1940.B1.

2   ROBB, NESCA ADELINE.  "Christina Rossetti" in
     Four in Exile.  London:  Hutchinson, pp.
     82-119.
        The main themes of Christina Rossetti's po-
     etry are the pain of love, the "betrayal of
     the dead by the living," and "the haunting of
     the living by the dead."  Christina Rossetti

1948

(ROBB, NESCA ADELINE)
is indebted to the Pre-Raphaelites for the
"ornate archaism" and the "sensuous element--
image, description, or technical device . . .
always, as it were, the body of the spiritual." The "Monna Innominata" sonnets,
"subtle and often noble in expression though
they are, convey little sense of a human relationship." Christina Rossetti "has sometimes been depicted as a kind of saintly ego-
ist, and it is true that the majority of her
poems are written in the first person, and
deal with the immediate relation of the soul
to its God or of one human heart to another."
Christina Rossetti sees death as "peace, a
suspension of all strife though not of all
consciousness. . . ."

1949 A   BOOKS

1    ZATURENSKA, MARYA. Christina Rossetti: A Por-
     trait with Background. New York: Macmillan.
     311 pp.
        Throughout the work Zaturenska combines
     biographical information with critical assess-
     ment of Christina Rossetti's poetry and prose.
     Chapter IV is an account of Christina
     Rossetti's antipathy toward Elizabeth Siddal,
     Dante Gabriel's wife. Zaturenska bases her
     view of Christina Rossetti's poetry, espe-
     cially "Goblin Market," on Violet Hunt's ac-
     count of Christina Rossetti's attempted elope-
     ment with James Collinson.

1949 B   SHORTER WRITINGS

1    ANON. "The Romantic World of the Rossettis,"
     New York Times Book Review (20 November), 3,
     37.

# Christina Rossetti: A Reference Guide

(ANON.)
Christina Rossetti is described as "quiet
and dusky and small," who "quivered away from
the soiling touch of quotidian reality" by
withdrawing into a dreamworld. "Goblin Market" is a "masterpiece" representative of
Christina Rossetti's own struggle with "pleasure, pride and self-indulgence."

2  BOWRA, C. M. "Christina Rossetti" in The Romantic Imagination. Cambridge, Mass.: Harvard
University Press, pp. 245-70.
"In her we see a truly Romantic temperament,
trained to look for beauty in mysterious
realms of experience, and able to find it
without any strain or forcing of herself."
Christina Rossetti's twofold nature is reflected in the twofold character of her poetry. On the one hand is the Pre-Raphaelite
poetry of imagination and fancy, and on the
other hand is the grave, serious poetry re-
flecting her inner life, as in many of her
devotional pieces. "Eve" maintains a balance
between the two. Love with Christina Rossetti
was strongly associated with death, as seen in
"Remember." The poetry reflects the conflict
between the woman and the saint in her. The
more serious Christina Rossetti is the less
she adorns her verse with images or preten-
tious words, yet she can build up to a climax
of "dazzling splendour" when she so desires,
as in the poem entitled "In Progress." Her
poetry was ultimately an escape from, as well
as a comment on, her own troubles.

3  DOUGHTY, OSWALD. Dante Gabriel Rossetti: A Vic-
torian Romantic. New Haven, Conn.: Yale
University Press, 712 pp.
Although Doughty's primary concern is with
Christina Rossetti's brother, his book

1949

(DOUGHTY, OSWALD)
includes interpretations of several of Christina Rossetti's poems. He interprets "Look
on This Picture and on This," for example, as
expressing Dante Gabriel Rossetti's suffering
due to his love for Elizabeth Siddal and concomitant infatuation with one of his models,
Annie Miller. "In an Artist's Studio" de-
picts Elizabeth Siddal's declining health.
Doughty believes (p. 289) that "The Prince's
Progress" could well be taken "for an allegorical description of the relations of
Gabriel and Lizzie during the preceding ten
years," that is, the years preceding their
marriage in 1860.

1953 A   BOOKS - NONE

1953 B   SHORTER WRITINGS

   1    IRONSIDE, ROBIN. "Introduction" in Poems by
Christina Rossetti. London: Grey Walls
Press, pp. 1-18.
After providing a brief biographical sketch,
Ironside notes that the "time had grown old
in which she truly grieved before any actual
calamity had befallen her; and if we may sug-
gest that the force of the poetry written in
her eighteenth year was due to the consciousness of womanhood, we may also feel that the
personal urgency with which she then handled
the same melancholy thoughts as had engrossed
her childhood was due to a ripened awareness
of how she herself must needs respond to the
poison of experience when called upon to drink
it" (pp. 4-5).

   2    WOOLF, VIRGINIA. A Writer's Diary: Being Extracts from the Diary of Virginia Woolf, ed.

(WOOLF, VIRGINIA)
   Leonard Woolf.  London:  Hogarth Press, p. 1.
   On p. 1 of her diary (1918) Virginia Woolf
describes Christina Rossetti as a "born poet"
who made "all her poetry subservient to the
Christian doctrines.  Consequently, as I
think, she starved into austere emaciation a
very fine original gift, which only wanted
licence to take to itself a far finer form
than, shall we say, Mrs. Browning's."


1955 A   BOOKS

   1    SAWTELL, MARGARET.  Christina Rossetti:  Her
        Life and Religion.  London:  A. R. Mowbray.
        160 pp.
           According to Sawtell, "This book has been
        written with the express purpose of clearing
        her name from the accusations of morbidity
        and self-torture" ("Preface," p. 7).  Some
        main themes of Christina Rossetti's poetry
        which are considered in this study are the
        sovereignty of love, the difference between
        love human and divine, the longing for rest
        in sleep, and renunciation.  Sawtell, like
        William Michael Rossetti, believes that
        Christina Rossetti was preoccupied during the
        late forties and fifties with memories of her
        affair with James Collinson.  In Chapter V
        Sawtell writes that such poems as the fragment
        of "A Nightmare," "A Birthday," "An Apple
        Gathering," and "Winter:  My Secret" show
        Christina Rossetti brooding over her love for
        Collinson (pp. 51-58).

   2    SHALKHAUSER, MARIAN DORIS.  The Poetry and Prose
        of Christina Rossetti.  Dissertation, Univer-
        sity of Wisconsin.  930 pp.

1955

(SHALKHAUSER, MARIAN DORIS)
The first part of this dissertation deals
with such prominent themes as self-sacrifice
and love human and divine; the second half of
the dissertation discusses the forms which
Christina Rossetti used most often, such as
sonnets, ballads, and short stories.

1955 B   SHORTER WRITINGS

1   GARLITZ, BARBARA.  "Christina Rossetti's Sing-
Song and Nineteenth-Century Children's Poetry," PMLA, LXX (June), 539-43.
In this article, Garlitz notes that "at
least half the poems are rooted in the moral
tradition of children's poetry. . . ."

2   HATTON, GWYNNETH.  "Introduction" in "An Edition
of the Unpublished Poems of Christina Rossetti,
With a Critical Introduction and Interpreta-
tive Notes to All the Posthumous Poems."  Masters essay, Oxford University, pp. vii-xciv.
Hatton describes the problems encountered by
Christina Rossetti when she began to publish
her volumes of poetry and analyzes the principles of editing which Christina Rossetti
practiced in preparing her volumes for publication.  She was extremely conscientious and
aware of the poet's responsibility toward his
readers; sometimes she omitted poems which she
felt were too personal or possibly offensive
to some readers.  In conclusion Hatton explains the organization of the texts of Christina Rossetti's unpublished poems which follow.

3   JARVIS, KATHLEEN.  "Introduction" in Poems of
Christina Rossetti.  London:  A. R. Mowbray,
pp. v-viii.
Christina Rossetti is compared with Alice
Meynell, a contemporaneous poet, whose poetry
was less "'inward-looking'" than Christina
Rossetti's.  Jarvis notes:  "Critics have
sometimes remarked upon Christina's unwhole-

(JARVIS, KATHLEEN)
some dwelling upon death. In order that we may the more fully understand her poetry it is necessary for us to realize that our present knowledge of medicine and surgery would probably have diagnosed her complaint and cured it. In the absence of this knowledge, Christina was obliged to regard herself as incurable. If we fail to understand this, we alienate ourselves from her poetry, unaware that here was a winged spirit soaring above and beyond its earthly pain-racked frame."

1956 A    BOOKS - NONE

1956 B    SHORTER WRITINGS

1    CLARKE, AUSTIN. "Christina Rossetti," Spectator, CXCVI (6 January), 27.
Clarke notes that Christina Rossetti's "carols were equally remarkable for she gave to a simple form a complex metrical pattern and her stanzas have the colour of Italian painting."

2    ELLIOTT-BINNS, L. E. English Thought, 1860-1900: The Theological Aspect. London: Longmans, Green and Co., pp. 13, 252-53.
In describing the theological atmosphere of the second half of the nineteenth century, Elliott-Binns quotes Christina Rossetti's letters and poetry in his discussion of the emotional appeals of theology, as well as the importance of the concept of life on earth as an "'ante-room to heaven.'"

3    JONES, HOWARD MUMFORD. "The Pre-Raphaelites" in The Victorian Poets: A Guide to Research, ed. Frederic E. Faverty. Cambridge, Mass.: Harvard University Press, pp. 161-95.
Christina Rossetti receives rather sporadic treatment in the conspectus of Pre-Raphaelite scholarship. Jones concludes, "As for Christina, she is virtually reduced to a World's

1957

(JONES, HOWARD MUMFORD)
Classics edition of The Goblin Market, The
Prince's Progress and Other Poems, and to two
editions of Sing-Song for juveniles" (Macmillan's Little Library Series, discontinued in
1955, and Macmillan's New Little Library Series, which began in 1953). The second edition of The Victorian Poets (See 1968.B3) contains an entire chapter devoted to Christina
Rossetti.

4    SHALKHAUSER, MARIAN. "The Feminine Christ," VN,
X (Autumn), 19-20.
"Christina Rossetti's 'Goblin Market' is a
unique Christian fairy tale in which a feminine cast of characters is substituted for
the masculine cast of the Biblical sin-redemp-
tion sequence. Lizzie, the pure sister, is
the symbol of Christ; Laura represents Adam-
Eve and consequently all of sinful mankind."

1957 A   BOOKS

1    PACKER, LONA MOSK. Beauty for Ashes: A Biographical Study of Christina Rossetti's Poetry. Dissertation, University of California.
This dissertation provided the basis for the
1963 biography (See 1963.A1).
In the intervening years Packer was able to
fill out the dissertation and document it more
carefully, but the basic thesis and structure
of the two works are the same.

1957 B   SHORTER WRITINGS

1    FAIRCHILD, HOXIE NEALE. "Christina Rossetti" in
Religious Trends in English Poetry, Volume IV,
1830-1880: Christianity and Romanticism in
the Victorian Era. New York: Columbia University Press, pp. 302-16.
Of Christina Rossetti, Fairchild observes,
"A less meticulous craftsman than Gabriel, she
is a better poet because she writes with her

(FAIRCHILD, HOXIE NEALE)
heart's blood rather than with ink." Christina longed for death as a release from "the
tension between what she was and what she
thought she should be."

1958 A   BOOKS - NONE

1958 B   SHORTER WRITINGS

1      PACKER, LONA MOSK. "Symbol and Reality in
Christina Rossetti's Goblin Market," PMLA
LXXIII (September), 375-85.
Packer feels that "Goblin Market" is
grounded in Christina Rossetti's own passions
and emotional experiences, especially her love
for William Bell Scott, which was frustrated
by his marriage to Alice Boyd.

1959 A   BOOKS - NONE

1959 B   SHORTER WRITINGS

1      ANON. "Not All Roses in the Victorian Nursery,"
TLS:  Children's Books (29 May), xi.
The reviewer of Speaking Likenesses notes,
"Judged by any standard, this is a peculiarly
revolting book, though . . . its nastiness is
mitigated by the framework in which it is set.
Nevertheless, the feeling of depression which
the reader undergoes is increased by the graph-
ic skill and imaginative power of the writer.
Possibly Speaking Likenesses is of more interest to Freudian psychology than literary
criticism."

2      LEWIS, NAOMI. "Introduction" in Christina
Rossetti (Pocket Poets). London:  Edward
Hulton, pp. 5-10.
"Her poems look simple enough, yet it is baf-
fling to see how, without searching, without
imagery almost, they embody time and again the
piercing inexpressible idea.  Paradoxically,
her lack of living experience seems to add a

119

1959

(LEWIS, NAOMI)
depth to her work. After all, the less one
tastes of experience the greater is its mystery; and mystery, the sense of the undiscov-
ered, runs through and through the poems."

3    PACKER, LONA MOSK. "Speaking Likenesses," TLS
(5 June), 337.
In this reply to "Not All Roses in the Victorian Nursery" (See 1959.B1), Packer quotes
from letters by Christina Rossetti on this
book:  the first title ("Nowhere," rejected
because of its similarity to Erewhon), was
changed to "Speaking Likenesses," or "embodi-
ments or caricatures of themselves or their
faults." Packer believes that Christina
Rossetti's illness of 1870-1872 provides a
simpler clue than "Freudian psychology" to the
so-called "strain of morbidity" in the story.

4    _____. "The Protestant Existentialism of Christina Rossetti," N&Q, CCIV (June), 213-15.
The two attributes of twentieth-century
"Protestant Existentialism" which also char-
acterize Christina Rossetti's outlook are a
recognition of the need for total commitment
(seen in "The Thread of Life"), and the relation between faith and personal identity, illustrated in The Face of the Deep.

1960 A  BOOKS

1    SWANN, THOMAS BURNETT. Wonder and Whimsey:  The
Fantastic World of Christina Rossetti. Fran-
cestown, New Hampshire:  Marshall Jones.  111
pp.
Swann's thesis is that Christina Rossetti
was both excellent and unique only in her
"fantastic" poems, such as the fantasies contained in Sing-Song. The source of these

1960

(SWANN, THOMAS BURNETT)
    poems is <u>wonder</u> (that which is strange and
    astonishing), and <u>whimsey</u> (that which is
    quaintly charming).  In the opening chapter
    Swann compares Christina Rossetti's poetry
    with that of her brother and other Pre-
    Raphaelites.  Swann discusses the similarities
    in the use of supernatural elements and con-
    crete, sensuous imagery.  Although Dante
    Gabriel was the better craftsman of the two,
    Christina's "very artlessness is the first
    prerequisite for whimsey" (pp. 24-25).  Chap-
    ter II discusses Christina Rossetti's animal
    and flower personifications.  Her humanized
    animals are drawn with a "half-serious pur-
    pose"; they illustrate human failings with
    greater subtlety than do those of Aesop or La
    Fontaine (p. 35).  Swann considers "A Frog's
    Fate" and "A Bird's Eye View" failures, due
    to sententiousness in the first and "whimsey
    turned grotesque" in the second (p. 43).
    Chapter III deals with a few of the best fan-
    tasies from <u>Sing-Song</u>, and likens her portray-
    als of elves, fairies, and flowers to the
    whimsey in some of Herrick's poems (pp.
    52-55).  Swann then discusses Christina's
    imitation of Lewis Carroll in <u>Speaking Like-</u>
    <u>nesses</u>, which Swann considers a failure.  In
    Chapter IV he analyzes four ghost poems ani-
    mated by wonder.  Chapter V is concerned with
    the long fantastic poems besides "Goblin Mar-
    ket"; that is, "The Months: A Pageant," "The
    Prince's Progress," and others.  In "The
    Prince's Progress" the prince and princess
    "procrastinate rather than come to grips with
    life," and as such are "probably projections
    of Christina's own recurrent fear that she
    herself had failed to live" (p. 81).  Swann
    notes the parallels in meter, story, and

1960

(SWANN, THOMAS BURNETT)
description between "From House to Home" and
Tennyson's "Palace of Art." "From House to
Home" is "another dramatization of Christina's
perpetual inner-warfare between earth and
heaven" (p. 86). The final chapter deals
with Christina Rossetti's "masterpiece," as
Swann terms "Goblin Market," which, "like a
child's daydream . . . is both terrifying and
unspeakably beautiful" (p. 93). Swann sees
the conflict between the goblins and Lizzie
and Laura as representative of "a conflict
between civilization and nature" (p. 95). He
compares "Goblin Market" to "The Forsaken
Merman" by Matthew Arnold--the former illus-
trating "intuitive wonder," the latter a work
of "conscious wonder" (p. 97). A bibliography
(pp. 109-11) concludes the book.

1960 B    SHORTER WRITINGS

1      RICKS, CHRISTOPHER. "'O Where Are You Going?'":
       W. H. Auden and Christina Rossetti," N&Q, CCV
       (December), 472.
            Ricks notes Auden's indebtedness in the
       opening of The Orators to "Amor Mundi," which
       was in an anthology co-edited by Auden in 1932
       (Poets of the English Language). Both poems
       are built upon the same structure of ques-
       tions. The similarities are most striking in
       the fourth stanza of "Amor Mundi."

1961 A    BOOKS - NONE

1961 B    SHORTER WRITINGS

1      BOWRA, C. M. "Christina Rossetti" in The Roman-
       tic Imagination. New York: Oxford Univer-

1962

(BOWRA, C. M.)
     sity Press, pp. 245-70.
     Reprint of 1949.B2.

1962 A  BOOKS - NONE

1962 B  SHORTER WRITINGS

1     DINGLEY, STANFORD.  "Translator's Preface" in
      Familiar Correspondence Newly Translated from
      the Italian of Christina G. Rossetti.  The
      Mill House Press, Stanford Dingley, pp. i-iii.
        Dingley quotes William Michael Rossetti's
      description of the Corrispondenza Famigliare
      (from The Poetical Works, p. 493):  "'In
      1851-52 some young ladies (mostly living in
      the Regent's Park neighbourhood) had a fancy
      for getting up a little privately-printed
      magazine, which was termed The Bouquet from
      Marylebone Gardens.  My sister was invited
      to contribute, and she consented to do so,
      writing always in Italian.  Each contributor
      adopted some floral name as a signature;
      Christina was "Calta".  . . .  Christina's
      principal contribution was in prose, not
      verse--a Corrispondenza Famigliare between
      two supposed young ladies, Italian and Eng-
      lish, the former being at school.'"  Dingley
      observes, "A pleasant and clever writer of
      fiction was lost in Christina Rossetti:  lost,
      but never to be regretted.  The translation
      and printing of these letters are to be jus-
      tified only as the presentation of an all but
      unknown work of a great poet."

2     PACKER, LONA MOSK.  "F. S. Ellis and the
      Rossettis:  A Publishing Venture and Misad-
      venture, 1870," WHR, XVI (Summer), 243-53.

1962

(PACKER, LONA MOSK)
This article quotes the letters from Dante
Gabriel to Christina Rossetti which influ-
enced her to change publishers from Macmillan
to Ellis, in order to be included in the co-
terie of poets, including Dante Gabriel
Rossetti and William Bell Scott, published by
Ellis.


1963 A   BOOKS

1      PACKER, LONA MOSK.  Christina Rossetti.
       Berkeley:  University of California Press.
       xx + 459 pp.
           In this biography, which is based on many
       previously unused letters, manuscripts, and
       notebook excerpts, Packer comes to a new con-
       clusion as to the subject of the mysterious
       love poems of the late fifties:  she believes
       that William Bell Scott was the third, and
       most important, man in Christina Rossetti's
       life, although there is little factual evi-
       dence to support her thesis.  She frequently
       uses Christina Rossetti's poetry to assist in
       her interpretation of Christina Rossetti's
       "inner life."  The book includes a reprint of
       1958.B1 and 1962.B2.


1963 B   SHORTER WRITINGS

1      BLUEN, HERBERT.  "The Poetry of Christina
       Rossetti,"  The Aryan Path (Bombay),
       (February), 79–83.
           Bluen describes Christina Rossetti as a
       "deeply religious" woman, and summarizes one
       of her "most remarkable" poems, "Goblin Mar-
       ket."  Bluen also quotes from "Remember,"
       "Winter;  My Secret," "Twilight Calm," "Shut

(BLUEN, HERBERT)
Out," "Rest," and "Up-Hill." He finds her
poems "like a peaceful garden full of singing
birds wherein we may find respite from the
clamours and perplexities of this atomic age."

2    PACKER, LONA MOSK. "Preface" and "Introduction"
in The Rossetti-Macmillan Letters: Some 133
Unpublished Letters Written to Alexander Macmillan, F. S. Ellis, and Others, by Dante
Gabriel, Christina, and William Michael
Rossetti, 1861-1889. Berkeley: University
of California Press, pp. v-ix, 1-9.

Packer notes that the sixty-eight letters
from Christina Rossetti reveal a businesslike
concern for the preparation of her books for
publication, retaining copyright, and revising
poems. They also reveal Christina Rossetti's
"courteous deference, playfulness, subtle in-
sight, and feminine wit." The "Introduction"
includes Ruskin's note containing a negative
verdict on "Goblin Market," as well as Macmillan's letter to Dante Gabriel Rossetti
stating his willingness to publish Goblin Market and Other Poems.

3    _____. "Swinburne and Christina Rossetti:
Atheist and Anglican." UTQ, XXXIII (October),
30-42.

This article describes the apparently in-
congruous friendship of Swinburne and Christina Rossetti. Although each admired the
other's poetry, Christina Rossetti was dis-
tressed by Swinburne's atheism, and Swinburne
was irritated by Christina Rossetti's devotional poetry, although Swinburne's admiration for Christina Rossetti is evinced in the
memorial poem he wrote at her death, entitled
"A New Year's Eve," which Packer quotes in

1963

> (PACKER, LONA MOSK)
> part (See 1895.B33 for annotation of "A New
> Year's Eve").

## 1964 A    BOOKS - NONE

## 1964 B    SHORTER WRITINGS

1    MURCIAUX, C. "Christina Rossetti: La Vierge
Sage des Préraphaélites," Revue de Paris
(December), 74-84.
    Christina Rossetti's poems reflect the
style and goals of the Pre-Raphaelites, by
whom she was surrounded. Her poetry expresses the spiritual fervor of the Renais-
sance. "Goblin Market" is praised for its
psychological subtlety. Dante Gabriel's
women—languid, morbid, tragic beauties
("chastes et voluptueuses")—sing in Christina Rossetti's poetry songs of enchanting
melancholy. In a voice childlike in its pur-
ity and clarity she sings, "too late for
love," the song of the "Vierges Sages."

## 1965 A    BOOKS

1    BATTISCOMBE, GEORGINA. Christina Rossetti,
Writers and Their Work Pamphlet No. 189.
London: Longmans and Green. 39 pp.
    A detailed description of Christina
Rossetti's background and parents, contrasting
the Italian and English strains in her family,
is followed by an account of her life. Chap-
ter II traces the influence of the Pre-
Raphaelite and Oxford Movements on Christina
Rossetti's writings, and discusses the extent
to which Christina Rossetti's poems reflect

(BATTISCOMBE, GEORGINA)
her own experiences. Packer's thesis remains
"'not proven'" (p. 19). Battiscombe uses
"The Heart Knoweth Its Own Bitterness" to
substantiate her theory that "it was not the
nature but the inadequacy of the demands of
the flesh which made her turn away to another
love" (p. 21). Christina Rossetti therefore
sought divine love, yet, as Maurice Bowra has
noted, her poetry reflects the constant tension between her human self and her divine
calling. Battiscombe notes that the strongest
influence on Christina Rossetti's poetry was
her brother Dante Gabriel Rossetti, who was
her "chief critic" (p. 34).

1965 B  SHORTER WRITINGS

1    FREDEMAN, WILLIAM E.  "Christina Georgina
     Rossetti" in Pre-Raphaelitism: A Biblio-
     cricital Study. Cambridge, Mass.: Harvard
     University Press, Section 44, pp. 176-82.
        Fredeman prefaces his lists of Christina
     Rossetti's works and the biography and criti-
     cism with a brief critical essay in which he
     notes that the "secular and spiritual conflict
     with which Christina wrestled is dramatically
     demonstrated in the two extremes of her
     poetry. . . ."

2    LYNDE, RICHARD D.  "A Note on the Imagery in
     Christina Rossetti's 'A Birthday,'" VP, III
     (Autumn), 261-63.
        Lynde believes that an examination of "the
     natural and artificially made objects which
     it ["A Birthday"] embodies will provide a fas-
     cinating glimpse into the associative method
     of the mind which produced it." Lynde finds
     numerous associations with the Bible, the

1965

(LYNDE, RICHARD D.)
world of trade in Victorian England, and some
of Dante Gabriel's paintings reflected in the
poem.

3    WEATHERS, WINSTON. "Christina Rossetti:  The
Sisterhood of Self," VP, III (Spring), 81-89.
In this article Weathers examines some of
Christina Rossetti's poems in the light of
the thesis that one of her major motifs "is
that of the fragmented self moving or strug-
gling toward harmony and balance."  He feels
that each of the two sisters in "Goblin Market" comprises part of a fragmented personality which in the end gains a wholeness and
maturity when both of the sisters marry and
thus take up "their appropriate tasks and op-
erations within the larger integrity of sisterhood itself."  The poems which show the
divided self are of three kinds:  "those that
simply analyze the self into its parts, those
that present the conflict within the self,
and those that deal with some sort of integra-
tion of self."  The remainder of the article
gives specific examples of these kinds of
poems, and concludes with the hope that Christina Rossetti will be viewed as "a serious,
masterful eschatological and psychological
poet" who was able to transcend the "simply
autobiographical and environmental statement
in her myth."

1966 A  BOOKS

1    JUHNKE, ANNA KREIDER.  Dante Gabriel and Christina Rossetti:  The Poetry of Love, Death,
and Faith.  Dissertation, Indiana University.
463 pp.

(JUHNKE, ANNA KREIDER)
The study shows the interrelationship between love, faith, and death, as Christina
Rossetti waited for delayed fulfillment of
love which was never realized. Her best
poems are those expressing the theme of "hope
deferred."

## 1966 B   SHORTER WRITINGS

1    EVANS, B. IFOR.  "Christina Georgina Rossetti"
in English Poetry in the Later Nineteenth Cen-
tury, 2nd edition, revised.  Chatham, England:
Mackey, pp. 87–103.
This is basically a reprint of 1933.B3, but
Evans updates the sketch of Christina
Rossetti's life by including a consideration
of Packer's 1963 biography of Christina
Rossetti.

## 1967 A   BOOKS – NONE

## 1967 B   SHORTER WRITINGS

1    COUGHLAN, SISTER JEREMY.  "Pre-Raphaelitism in
the Poetry of Christina Rossetti" in The Pre-
Raphaelite Aesthetic and the Poetry of Christina Rossetti, William Morris, and William
Butler Yeats.  Dissertation, University of
Minnesota, pp. 37–81.
Coughlan shows how Christina Rossetti's poetry is Pre-Raphaelite in its truth to nature,
its mass of insignificant details, and its
use of prose rhythms in poetry.

1968

## 1968 A  BOOKS

1   BAUMBACH, F. E.  Relativity and Polarity in
        Christina Rossetti.  Dissertation, University
        of Wisconsin.  147 pp.
          This is an examination of the effects of
        Christina Rossetti's dependence upon religion
        for a synthesis in every personal dilemma, as
        well as in her poetry.

2   WILKINSON, DAVID CARL.  "Death in Love and Life
        in Death:  A Comparison of Major Themes in
        the Early Poetry of Dante Gabriel Rossetti
        and Christina Rossetti."  Masters essay, Uni-
        versity of Texas, pp. 25-47.
          Christina Rossetti's treatment of love is
        more circumspect than is Dante Gabriel's.
        Dante Gabriel sees love as giving life its
        significance, while Christina Rossetti sees
        religious devotion as the essence of life.

## 1968 B  SHORTER WRITINGS

1   BOYLE, SIR EDWARD.  "Christina Rossetti" in Bio-
        graphical Essays, 1790-1890.  Freeport, New
        York:  Books for Libraries Press, 193-203.
        Reprint of 1936.B1.

2   BUCKLEY, JEROME H.  "Christina Rossetti (1830-
        1894)," in The Pre-Raphaelites (Modern
        Library College Editions).  New York:  Random
        House, pp. 197-98.
          Buckley discussed briefly Christina
        Rossetti's part in the Pre-Raphaelite Move-
        ment.  She "was from the beginning both close
        to the center of the Pre-Raphaelite movement
        and at the same time, in her quiet asceticism,
        aloof from its bohemian exuberance."  He also
        notes that Christina Rossetti's secular poems

# CHRISTINA ROSSETTI: A REFERENCE GUIDE

1968

(BUCKLEY, JEROME H.)
". . . reflect a Pre-Raphaelite response to
sharp outline and vivid color and a delight
in detail that takes on a symbolic force."
Thirty-seven of Christina Rossetti's poems
are reprinted here (pp. 198-256), including
"Dream Land," "Rest," "After Death," "A Birth
Birthday," "An Apple-Gathering," "The Convent
Threshold," "Up-Hill," "Goblin Market," and
the "Monna Innominata" sonnets.

3    FREDEMAN, WILLIAM E.   "The Pre-Raphaelites.
Christina Rossetti" in <u>The Victorian Poets</u>:
<u>A Guide to Research</u>, ed. Frederic E. Faverty.
2nd ed.   Cambridge, Mass.:   Harvard University Press, pp. 284-93.
Unlike the first edition (<u>See</u> 1956.B3), the
second edition contains an entire chapter devoted to Christina Rossetti, accurately re-
flecting the growing interest taken in her
life and work during the intervening twelve
years.   Fredeman summarizes and evaluates the
biography, criticism, and critical editions
of the poetry and letters of Christina
Rossetti.   In Fredeman's opinion Mackenzie
Bell and Lona Mosk Packer have written the
best biographies thus far.   He concludes by
noting the need for a definitive edition of
Christina Rossetti's poetry as well as her
correspondence.

4    DeVITAS, A. A.   "<u>Goblin Market</u>:   Fairy Tale and
Reality," <u>JPC</u>, I (Spring), 418-26.
DeVitas sees "Goblin Market" as allegorical-
ly expressive of "the means by which the artist apprehends beauty" even though it may be
a mask of evil in reality.   Thus the artist
must be strong and practical-minded enough to
face the reality of evil, but must also be

(DeVITAS, A. A.)
   imaginative and sensitive to the beauty which
   may hide that reality.

5    KOHL, JAMES A.  "A Medical Comment on Christina
       Rossetti," N&Q, CCXIII (November), 423-24.
       This note reprints a handwritten statement
   that Christina Rossetti was found to be suffering from "'a kind of religious mania'" by
   her physician (Dr. Hare) when she was 16-18
   years old.  This could explain in part her
   intense periods of melancholy, and it con-
   firms the alleged religious reasons for re-
   jecting Collinson and Cayley while weakening
   Packer's theory that Christina Rossetti was
   in love with William Bell Scott.


1969 A  BOOKS

1    FESTA, CONRAD DANIEL.  Studies in Christina
       Rossetti's 'GOBLIN MARKET' AND OTHER POEMS.
       Dissertation, University of South Carolina.
       259 pp.
       Festa discusses three strands of Christina
   Rossetti's poetry:  the longer narrative
   poems, the secular lyrics, and some of the
   devotional poems--as they appear in the volume entitled Goblin Market and Other Poems.
   He draws parallels between the narratives and
   the Pre-Raphaelite poems of D. G. Rossetti
   and William Morris, and compares her devotional poems to those of George Herbert.

2    HÖNNIGHAUSEN, GISELA.  Christina Rossetti als
       viktorianische Dichterin.  Bonn.  363 pp.
       The book is not obtainable through the
   usual booksellers, since it was privately
   printed and financed through a special grant

1969

(HÖNNIGHAUSEN, GISELA)
    of the German industry, according to the au-
thor. Hönnighausen discusses Christina
Rossetti's "manifold literary output as an
expression of her Victorian frame of mind"
(quoting from her letter to R. W. Crump,
10 August 1974). The first two chapters analyze Christina Rossetti's use of poetic form
and her experiments with rhyme and meter.
Chapter III considers Christina Rossetti's religious prose and her relationship to the
Anglican Church. In Chapter IV Hönnighausen
places Christina Rossetti's children's verse,
especially her volume entitled Sing-Song, in
the context of nineteenth-century nonsense
verse. The fifth chapter is a treatment of
some of the allegorical and symbolic emblems
in Christina Rossetti's poetry, especially her
flower images. The final chapters, treating
of Christina Rossetti's religious poetry and
the atmosphere in her work, are followed by
an appendix containing several illustrations
taken from Christina Rossetti's volumes of
poetry.

3    KOHL, JAMES ALFRED. Sparks of Fire: Christina
      Rossetti's Artistic Life. Dissertation, Uni-
      versity of Delaware. 144 pp.
    The author divides Christina Rossetti's lit-
erary career into four periods and seeks to
relate her life to her poetry in each of the
periods, which are dated as follows: 1830-
1849, 1850-1866, 1867-1881, and 1882-1894. In
his conclusion Kohn writes, "Fixed by nature
in the habit of deep meditation and trained by
her interest in drawing and painting to notice
carefully her surroundings, Christina created
her poetry from the higher longings of the
whole race of man and expressed it in the

(KOHL, JAMES ALFRED)
simple and natural details of her own experience" (p. 120). The dissertation contains an
appendix giving the dates and locations of
Christina Rossetti's notebooks, and also an
appendix showing the correlation of published
and unpublished poems by her; she published
31 percent, or 135, of the 432 poems in her
extant notebooks.

4    UFFELMAN, LARRY KENT.  Christina Rossetti's A
PAGEANT AND OTHER POEMS:  An Annotated Critical Edition.  Dissertation, Kansas State University.  295 pp.
The work is divided into two parts:  the
text of A Pageant and Other Poems, which comprises the second part, is preceded by a critical survey of the scholarship concerning
Christina Rossetti, a description of the literary movements which affected her poetry,
particularly the Oxford Movement and the Pre-
Raphaelite Movement, and a consideration of
the leading themes in her poetry.  Uffelman
notes the overabundance of biographies and
the scarcity of textual and interpretive studies of her writings.

1969 B   SHORTER WRITINGS

1    LEWIS, NAOMI.  "Introduction" in Christina
Rossetti, Doves and Pomegranates:  Poems for
Young Readers, Chosen by David Powell, Illustrated by Margery Gill.  London:  Bodley Head,
pp. 5-13.
Lewis gives an account of Christina
Rossetti's life and describes each of her
brothers and her sister Maria.  After summa-
rizing "Goblin Market" and noting the popular-
ity of such poems as "What is Pink?" from

# CHRISTINA ROSSETTI: A REFERENCE GUIDE

1969

(LEWIS, NAOMI)
Sing-Song, Lewis concludes: "But at her best,
Christina Rossetti can catch in what seems
the lightest possible way some piercing, almost inexpressible idea, and make it seem a
revelation of our own unrealised thoughts."

2    PACKER, LONA MOSK. "Rossetti, Christina Georgina" in Collier's Encyclopedia, 24 vols.
New York: Crowell-Collier Educational Cor-
poration, XX, 225.
In giving a brief account of Christina
Rossetti's life, Packer suggests that Christina Rossetti loved William Bell Scott as well
as her two suitors, Collinson and Cayley.
Packer notes in conclusion that Christina
Rossetti's "literary reputation declined after
her death, but recent re-evaluations acknowl-
edge her pre-eminence among Victorian poets.
The profundity of idea and emotion in her most
powerful poems has seldom been questioned, but
the extent of her output (she wrote over a
thousand poems) and its range are wider than
has been supposed."

3    WALLER, JOHN O. "Christ's Second Coming: Christina Rossetti and the Premillennialist William
Dodsworth," BYNPL, LXXIII (September), 465-82.
Waller attempts to establish a relationship
between the sermons of William Dodsworth,
Curator of Christ's Church in Albany Street,
and Christina Rossetti's poems concerning
Christ's Second Coming. The article offers an
analysis of some of the thirty-five poems
which Christina Rossetti wrote on the Second
Coming.

135

# CHRISTINA ROSSETTI: A REFERENCE GUIDE

1970

## 1970 A  BOOKS

1    WEIDEMAN, REBECCA S.  A Critical Bibliography of
     Christina Rossetti.  Dissertation, University
     of Texas.  184 pp.
         The present bibliography is a revised and
     reorganized version of this dissertation.
     The dissertation is divided into three major
     sections which are annotated throughout:
     bibliographical aids, writings of Christina
     Rossetti (with reviews), and biography and
     criticism.

## 1970 B  SHORTER WRITINGS

1    JENNINGS, ELIZABETH.  "Introduction" in A Choice
     of Christina Rossetti's Verse.  London:
     Faber and Faber, pp. 9–12.
         Jennings believes that Christina Rossetti
     was a "poet of unusual talent who was born at
     a time when it was difficult to write really
     great poetry."  While she is not a major
     poet, Christina Rossetti is "certainly in the
     forefront of minor late nineteenth-century
     English poets."

2    OWEN, MARION.  "Christina Rossetti:  'Affairs of
     the Heart,'" HAB, XXI (Summer), 16–25.
         Owen gives a description of Christina
     Rossetti's two suitors, James Collinson and
     Charles Cayley, and a summary of Lona Mosk
     Packer's thesis that Christina Rossetti loved
     a third man, William Bell Scott.  After ques-
     tioning Packer's interpretation of Christina
     Rossetti's love poems, Owen agrees with
     Christina Rossetti's brother, William Michael
     Rossetti, that Christina Rossetti loved only
     two men:  "James Collinson and--most of all--
     Charles Bagot Cayley."

3    ZATURENSKA, MARYA. "Introduction: The passion-
     ate Austerity of Christina Rossetti" in Se-
     lected Poems of Christina Rossetti. London
     and New York: Macmillan, pp. 3-17.
        A description of Christina Rossetti's Ital-
     ian and English heritage is followed by a dis-
     cussion of her love poetry. "An Italian fer-
     vor firmly held within a strict Church of
     England orthodoxy gave her devotional verse
     its exotic flavor and also resulted in some of
     the most beautiful poems in the English lan-
     guage--passionate in their feeling, delicate
     in their undercurrent of sensuality, and very
     Latin in their often erotic mysticism."


1971 A   BOOKS

1    COOK, WISTER JEAN. The Sonnets of Christina
     Rossetti: A Comparative Prosodic Analysis.
     Dissertation, Auburn University. 305 pp.
        Cook analyzes the metrics of Christina
     Rossetti's sonnets and compares her experi-
     mental techniques to those of other sonnet
     writers, namely, Dante Gabriel Rossetti,
     Algernon Swinburne, and George Meredith.
     Christina Rossetti "exhibits a more marked
     leaning toward regularity than any of the
     other poets do," but on the other hand, "when
     she varies from the conventional iambic pen-
     tameter line, her variation from it is in most
     instances as extreme as her adherence to it"
     (p. 298). Cook concludes that "Rossetti's
     sonnets are models of smoothness; Meredith
     likes a rough, asymmetrical line; Swinburne
     dazzles with technical brilliance. Christina
     Rossetti, both when she emphasizes metrical
     and caesural variations and when she empha-
     sizes regularity of line, produces a neat,

(COOK, WISTER JEAN)
tight sonnet form characterized by strictly
defined metrical and syntactical patterns and
--with few exceptions--a strictly limited
line" (p. 301).

## 1971 B  SHORTER WRITINGS

1   CURRAN, STUART. "The Lyric Voice of Christina
Rossetti," VP, IX (Autumn), 287-99.
Curran notes that the weaknesses of Christina Rossetti's poetry are frequent sentimen-
tality and limited subject matter. "She has
only one real subject, mortality, and the variety of her treatment is never extensive."
Curran analyzes Christina Rossetti's "constant
experimentation" with the sonnet form and concludes his essay with the thought that Christina Rossetti had the "true lyric voice" of a
gifted minor poet.

2   KOHL, JAMES A. "Christina Rossetti's Il
Rosseggiar dell' Oriente," AntigR, II (Sum-
mer), 46-61.
Before giving the Italian text and his English translation side by side, Kohn describes
the work, Il Rosseggiar dell' Oriente (The
Reddening of the East) as "a group of twenty-
one poems composed intermittently between
December, 1862, and August, 1868." The poems
express Christina Rossetti's hope and eventual
disappointment concerning her engagement to
Charles Cayley, which was broken sometime
around 1866.

## 1972 A  BOOKS - NONE

## 1972 B    SHORTER WRITINGS

1    BRZENK, EUGENE J. "'Up-Hill' and 'Down-' by
        Christina Rossetti," VP, X (Winter), 367-71.
            Brzenk compares "Up-Hill" and "Amor Mundi,"
        showing that they are linked together by the
        common metaphor of life as a path or road.
        They also reflect the simplicity and direct-
        ness characteristic of folk literature.

2    CRUMP, R. W. "Eighteen Moments' Monuments:
        Christina Rossetti's Bouts-Rimés Sonnets in
        the Troxell Collection," PULC, XXXIII
        (Spring), 210-29.
            Eight of the eighteen poems have never be-
        fore appeared in print; the other ten are in-
        cluded in William Michael Rossetti's 1904 edi-
        tion of Christina Rossetti's poems. The ar-
        ticle includes facsimiles of two of the rough
        drafts in the Troxell Collection.

3    _____. "Eighteen Moments' Monuments: Christina
        Rossetti's Bouts-Rimés Sonnets in the Troxell
        Collection" in Essays on the Rossettis, ed.
        Robert S. Fraser. Princeton, New Jersey:
        Princeton University Press, pp. 210-29.
        Reprint of 1972.B2.

4    HERENDEEN, WARREN. "Andrew Marvell and Christina
        Rossetti," SCN, XXX (Spring), 8-9.
            In this brief article Herendeen demonstrates
        the similarities in Christina Rossetti's "Gob-
        lin Market" and Andrew Marvell's "The Garden"
        and "Bermudas." In all three poems the "sense
        of sensuous ripeness is comparable."

5    _____. "The Midsummer Eves of Shakespeare and
        Christina Rossetti," VN, No. XLI (Spring),
        24-26.

(HERENDEEN, WARREN)
Herendeen draws a parallel between the two
sisters in "Goblin Market" and Hermia and
Helena in A Midsummer Night's Dream. "Play
and poem echo each other in numerous ways,
none of which is sufficiently precise to be
called other than a possibly conscious
theft."

6   HÖNNIGHAUSEN, GISELA. "Emblematic Tendencies in
the Works of Christina Rossetti," VP, X
(Spring), 1-15.
The article is derived from Hönnighausen's
book-length study (See 1969.A2), particularly
Chapter V. After giving several examples of
the widespread emblematic tendencies of nineteenth-century literature, Hönnighausen describes the patterns of images and emblems
found in Christina Rossetti's poetry. Christina Rossetti's frequent use of flower images
is characteristic of "the Victorian love of
decoration and embellishment, which, in its
escapist character, reminds one of the flower
patterns of the Biedermeier period in Germany
(ca. 1815-1848)." Hönnighausen analyzes in
detail the flower imagery in "Goblin Market,"
"To My Fior-di-Lisa," and some of the poems
from Christina Rossetti's volume of children's
poetry, Sing-Song.

7   STEVENSON, LIONEL. "Christina Rossetti" in The
Pre-Raphaelite Poets. Chapel Hill, North
Carolina: University of North Carolina Press,
78-122.
In comparing Christina Rossetti with three
contemporaneous poets, Emily Brontë, Emily
Dickinson, and Elizabeth Barrett Browning,
Stevenson notes that "the love poems of all
four are a strange amalgam of frustrated

(STEVENSON, LIONEL)
passion and religious devotion, persistently
preoccupied with death." Stevenson believes
that the greatest quality of Christina
Rossetti's poetry is its lyricism. "By the
age of eighteen she had perfected her characteristic poetic manner. Her sonnets move
with a pellucid grace wholly different from
the ornateness in those of her brother." He
provides ample quotations from her poetry
throughout the essay.

1973 A    BOOKS - NONE

1973 B    SHORTER WRITINGS

1    DE GROOT, HANS B.    "Christina Rossetti's 'A
Nightmare': A Fragment Completed," <u>RES</u>, XXIV
(February), 48-52.
    The article provides a critical text of "A
Nightmare," based on the manuscripts at the
Princeton University Library and the British
Library, and a description of the manuscripts
of the poem. In a footnote he notes the
existence of a fair copy manuscript of an-
other poem, "A Year's Windfalls," now in the
Brown University Library, Providence, Rhode
Island.

# Author/Title Index

Age of Tennyson.  Handbooks of English Literature,
    1900.B3

Agresti-Rossetti, Olivia,  1906.B1

Ancient Lights,  1911.B4

"Andrew Marvell and Christina Rossetti," 1972.B4

Anne Gilchrist:  Her Life and Writings,  1887.B2

Anonymous articles,
    1862.B1, B2, B3, B4, B5, B6
    1864.B1
    1866.B1, B2, B3, B4, B5, B6, B7, B8
    1868.B1, B2
    1870.B1, B2
    1871.B1
    1872.B1, B2, B3
    1874.B1, B2
    1876.B1, B2
    1881.B1, B2, B3, B4, B5
    1882.B1
    1886.B1
    1887.B1
    1890.B1
    1892.B1
    1893.B1, B2, B3, B4
    1895.B1, B2, B3, B4, B5, B6, B7, B8, B9, B10

```
1896.B1, B2, B3, B4, B5, B6, B7, B8, B9
1898.B1, B2, B3, B4, B5, B6
1899.B1, B2, B3, B4
1904.B1, B2, B3, B4
1908.B1
1912.B1
1928.B1
1930.B1, B2, B3
1931.B1, B2, B3
1949.B1
1959.B1
```

Appreciation of the Late Christina G. Rossetti,  1899.A1

Armytage, A. J. Green,  1906.B2

Bald, Marjory A.,  1923.B1

Bardi, Pietro,  1933.B1

Barzia, Elspeth H.,  1890.B2

Bates, Katharine Lee,  1895.B11

Battiscombe, Georgina,  1965.A1

Battle of the Bays,  1896.B19

Baumbach, F. E.,  1968.A1

Beauty for Ashes:  A Biographical Study of Christina
    Rossetti's Poetry,  1957.A.1

Beerbohm, Max,  1922.B1

Bell, Mackenzie,
    1895.B12, B13
    1898.A1

Belloc, Elizabeth,  1942.B1

# AUTHOR/TITLE INDEX

Benson, Arthur Christopher,
   1895.B14, B15
   1896.B10

Betham-Edwards, Matilda Barbara,   1911.B1

Bibliography,
   1898.A1
   1931.A3
   1956.B3
   1960.A1
   1963.A1
   1965.B1
   1968.B3
   1970.A1

Biographical Essays, 1790-1890,
   1936.B1
   1968.B1

Biographies (book-length),
   1898.A1
   1899.A1
   1915.A1
   1923.A1, A2
   1930.A1, A3, A4
   1931.A1, A2, A3
   1932.A1
   1949.A1
   1955.A1
   1957.A1
   1965.A1

Birkhead, Edith,   1930.A1

Bluen, Herbert,   1963.B1

Boase, Frederic,   1901.B1

Book of Preferences in Literature,   1915.B1

Book of Sonnet Sequences,   1929.B2

Bourne, Anna Ruth, 1920.A1

Bowker, R. R., 1888.B1

Bowra, C. M.,
　·1949.B2
　1961.B1

Boyle, Sir Edward,
　1936.B1
　1968.B1

Breme, Mary Ignatia, 1907.A1

Brief Memoir of Christina G. Rossetti, 1895.A2

Broers, Bernarda Conradina, 1923.B2

Brown, E. K., 1942.B2

Browning, Elizabeth Barrett,
　1927.A1
　1939.A1

Brzenk, Eugene J., 1972.B1

Buck, Elizabeth Fleming, 1933.A1

Buckley, Jerome H., 1968.B2

Burke, Charles Bell, 1913.B1

Buys, R. Van Brakell, 1947.B1

Caine, T. Hall, 1881.B6

Called to Be Saints, 1881.B7

Cambridge History of English Literature,
　1917.B2
　1933.B6

Campaigner at Home,  1864.B1

Cary, Elisabeth Luther,  1900.B1

Catholic Spirit in Modern English Literature,  1922.B2

Cazamian, Madeleine,  1911.B2

Century of Roundels,  1833.B3

Chambers, Edmund K.,  1894.B1

Chambers's Cyclopaedia of English Literature
    1904.B9
    1938.B1

Channel Passage and Other Poems,  1904.B12

Chapman, Edward Mortimer,  1910.B1

Chaucer's Nuns, and Other Essays,  1925.B1

Choice of Christina Rossetti's Verse (Jennings),  1970.B1

Christina Georgina Rossetti (Thomas),  1931.A3

Christina Georgina Rossetti:  An Essay (Venkatesan),
    1914.B2

"Christina Georgina Rossetti:  A Study and Some Com-
    parisons,"  1930.B6

Christina Rossetti (Battiscombe),  1965.A1

Christina Rossetti (English Association Pamphlet No. 78),
    1931.A2

Christina Rossetti (English Men of Letters Series),
    1930.A4

Christina Rossetti (Lewis),  1959, B2

# CHRISTINA ROSSETTI: A REFERENCE GUIDE

Christina Rossetti (Packer), 1963.A1

"Christina Rossetti" (Teasdale), 1932.A1

Christina Rossetti: A Biographical and Critical Study
(Bell), 1898.A1

"Christina Rossetti: A Brief Survey of Her Life and
Poetry" (Martin), 1915.A1

"Christina Rossetti: 'Affairs of the Heart,'" 1970.B2

Christina Rossetti als Viktorianische Dichterin, 1969.A2

"Christina Rossetti and Emily Dickinson," 1930.B13

"Christina Rossetti and Her Critics" (Smith), 1934.A1

Christina Rossetti and Her Poetry (Birkhead), 1930A.1

Christina Rossetti: A Portrait with Background
(Zaturenska), 1949.A1

"Christina Rossetti: A Reconsideration," 1930.B7

"Christina Rossetti as Exponent of the English Pre-
Raphaelite Movement" (Bourne), 1920.A1

"Christina Rossetti: 'A Singer of Death'" (Stewart),
1933.A3

Christina Rossetti: A Study (Shove), 1931.A1

"Christina Rossetti, December 5, 1830; December 5, 1930,"
1930.B10

Christina Rossetti: Her Life and Religion (Sawtell),
1955.A1

"Christina Rossetti: La Vierge Sage des Préraphaélites," 1964.B1

Christina Rossetti: Poems (de la Mare), 1930.B4

Christina Rossetti, Poet and Woman (De Wilde), 1923.A2

"Christina Rossetti's 'A Nightmare': A Fragment Completed," 1973.B1

Christina Rossetti's A PAGEANT AND OTHER POEMS: An Annotated Critical Edition (Uffleman), 1969.A4

"Christina Rossetti's Contributions to Notes and Queries," 1928.B1

"Christina Rossetti's Il Rosseggiar dell' Oriente," 1971.B2

"Christina Rossetti's Sing-Song and Nineteenth-Century Children's Poetry," 1955.B1

"Christina Rossetti: The Poetess of the Oxford Movement," 1933.B5

"Christina Rossetti: The Sisterhood of Self," 1965.B3

"Christina Rossetti: The Two Christmastides,"
1895.B37
1906.B7

Christina Rossetti und der Einfluss der Bibel auf Ihre Dichtung: Eine Literarische-Stilistische Untersuchung, Münstersche Beiträge zur Englischen Literaturgeschichte, No. 4, 1907.A1

"Christ's Second Coming: Christina Rossetti and the Premillenialist William Dodsworth," 1969.B3

Clarke, Austin, 1956.B1

Clear, Claudius, See Nicoll, W. Robertson

Clutton-Brock, Arthur,
1927.B1
1928.B2

CHRISTINA ROSSETTI: A REFERENCE GUIDE

Coleridge, Christabel R., 1895.B16

Collier's Encyclopedia, 1969.B2

Colvin, Sidney, 1872.B4

Coming of Love, Rhona Boswell's Story, and Other Poems, 1906.B7

Commonplace and Other Short Stories,
 1870.B1, B2, B3
 1871.B1, B2
 1895.B28

"Comparison of Christina Rossetti and Emily Dickinson as Poets of the Inner Life" (Walters), 1931.A4

"Comparison of the Poetry of Christina Rossetti and Emily Dickinson" (Buck), 1933.A1

Complete Lectures: A History of English Literature, 1934.B2

Cook, Wister Jean, 1971.A1

Cooper, Thompson, 1879.B1

Coughlan, Sister Jeremy, 1967.B1

Courten, Maria Luisa Giartosio de, 1928.B3

Critical Bibliography of Christina Rossetti, 1970.A1

Critical Essays and Literary Notes, 1880.B1

Critical Kit-Kats, 1903.B1

Critical Studies (book-length),
 1907.A1
 1920.A1
 1923.A2
 1927.A1
 1929.A1

# Author/Title Index

(Critical Studies)
    1930.A1, A2
    1931.A1, A2, A4
    1933.A1, A2, A3
    1934.A1
    1955.A2
    1960.A1
    1966.A1
    1968.A1, A2
    1969.A1, A2, A3, A4
    1971.A1

Crump, R. W.,
    1972.B2, B3
    See also Weideman, Rebecca S.

Cunliffe, John W., 1934.B1

Curran, Stuart, 1971.B1

Dallas, Eneas Sweetland, 1865.B1

Dante Gabriel and Christina Rossetti: The Poetry of
    Love, Death, and Faith, 1966.A1

Dante Gabriel Rossetti: A Victorian Romantic, 1949.B3

Dante Gabriel Rossetti: His Family Letters, With a
    Memoir, 1895.B28, B29

Dear Prue's Husband and Other People, 1932.B5

"Death in Love and Life in Death: A Comparison of Major
    Themes in the Early Poetry of Dante Gabriel Rossetti
    and Christina Rossetti," 1968.A2

De Bary, Anna Bunston, 1912.B2

de Groot, Hans B., 1973.B1

De La Mare, Walter John,
    1926.B1
    1930.B4

Dennett, J. R., 1866.B9

DeVitas, A. A., 1968.B4

De Wilde, Justine Frederika, 1923.A2

Dickinson, Emily,
    1931.A4
    1933.A1

Dictionary of National Biography, 1897.B1

Dingley, Stanford, 1962.B1

Distinguished Women Writers, 1934.B3

Doughty, Oswald, 1949.B3

Doves and Pomegranates: Poems for Young Readers,
    1969.B1

Dramatis Personae, 1923.B3

Drie Dichteressen uit het Victoriaanse Tijdperk. Chris-
    tina Rossetti, Emily Brontë, Elizabeth Barrett
    Browning, 1947.B1

Dubslaff, Friedrich, 1933.A2

Dunbar, Olivia Howard, 1909.B1

"Edition of the Unpublished Poems of Christina Rossetti"
    (Hatton), 1955.B2

Eighteen-Eighties: Essays by Fellows of the Royal So-
    ciety of Literature, 1930.B11

"Eighteen Moments' Monuments: Christina Rossetti's
    Bouts-Rimés Sonnets in the Troxell Collection,"
    1972.B2, B3

Eliot, Ruth F., 1927.A1

"Elizabeth Barrett Browning and Christina G. Rossetti:
    A Comparative Study" (Highley), 1939.A1

"Elizabeth Barrett Browning and Christina Rossetti: A
    Comparison" (Eliot), 1927.A1

Elliott-Binns, L. E., 1956.B2

Ellis, S. M., 1930.B5

Elton, Oliver, 1920.B1

# Author/Title Index

"Emblematic Tendencies in the Works of Christina
  Rossetti," 1972.B6

English Authors:  A Handbook of English Literature from
  Chaucer to Living Writers,  1906.B6

English Literature:  An Illustrated Record in Four Volumes,  1904.B5

English Literature in Account with Religion, 1800-1900,
  1910.B1

English Poetesses:  A Series of Critical Biographies,
  1883.B1

English Poetry in the Later Nineteenth Century,  1933.B3

English Poetry in the Later Nineteenth Century (2nd ed.),
  1966.B1

English Poets:  Selections with Critical Introductions by
  Various Writers,  1918.B2

English Thought, 1860-1900:  The Theological Aspect,
  1956.B2

English Women,  1942.B3

Essai sur la Poésie Anglaise au XIX$^e$ Siècle,  1906.B4

Essays,  1896.B10

Essays by Diverse Hands,  1926.B1

Essays on the Rossettis,  1972.B3

Evans, B. Ifor,
    1933.B2, B3
    1966.B1

Ewing, Thomas J.,  1891.B1

153

CHRISTINA ROSSETTI: A REFERENCE GUIDE

Face of the Deep
    1892.B1
    1893.B2

Fairchild, Hoxie Neale,  1957.B1

Familiar Correspondence Newly Translated from the Italian
    of Christina G. Rossetti,  1962.B1

Family Letters of Christina Georgina Rossetti,  1909.B1

Faverty, Frederic E.,
    1956.B3
    1968.B3

"Feminine Christ,"  1956.B4

Festa, Conrad Daniel,  1969.A1

"Fettered Christina Rossetti,"  1932.B3

Field, Michael,  1896.B11

Forman, Harry Buxton,
    1869.B1
    1871.B2

Four in Exile,  1948.B2

Fredeman, William E.
    1965.B1
    1968.B3

Frend, Grace Gilchrist,  1929.B1.  See also Gilchrist,
    Grace

Friendly Faces of Three Nationalities,  1911.B1

"F. S. Ellis and the Rossettis:  A Publishing Venture and
    Misadventure, 1879,"  1962.B2

Garlitz, Barbara, 1955.B1

Garnett, Richard, 1897.B1

Gilchrist, Grace, 1896.B12. See also Frend, Grace
    Gilchrist

Gilchrist, Herbert Harlakenden, 1887.B2

"Goblin Market,"
    1933.B2
    1956.B4
    1958.B1
    1960.A1
    1965.B3
    1968.B4

Goblin Market and Other Poems,
    1862.B1, B2, B3, B4, B5, B6
    1863.B1, B2
    1864.B1
    1865.B1
    1867.B1
    1969.A1

"Goblin Market: Fairy Tale and Reality," 1968.B4

Goblin Market, The Prince's Progress and Other Poems
    (1875),
    1876.B1, B2
    1877.B1
    1883.B1
    1887.B1

Gosse, Edmund,
    1893.B5
    1895.B17
    1903.B1
    1904.B5

Goyau, L. Felix-Faure, 1906.B3

Grappe, Georges, 1906.B4

Grebanier, Frances [Frances Winwar],
    1933.B4
    1934.B4

Green, Zaidee Eudora, 1936.B2

Greene, Kathleen Conyngham, 1930.B6

Griswold, Hattie Tyng, 1898.B7

Hatton, Gwynneth, 1955.B2

Hearn, Lafcadio, 1934.B2

Herendeen, Warren, 1972.B4, B5

Highley, Mona Patrocinio, 1939.A1

Hinkson, Katharine Tynan
    1893.B6
    1895.B18, B19, B20
    1912.B5, B6

History of English Literature, and of the Chief English
    Writers, Founded upon the Manual of Thomas B. Shaw,
    1901.B3

History of English Prosody from the Twelfth Century to
    the Present Day, 1910.B3

Hönnighausen, Gisela
    1969.A2
    1972.B6

Hopkins, Gerard Manley, 1937.B1

Hubbard, Elbert, 1897.B2

Hudson, William Henry, 1918.B1

# Author/Title Index

Hueffer, Ford Madox,
    1904.B6, B7
    1911.B3, B4, B5

Hundred Poems (by William Watson),    1922.B3

"Hundred Years Ago:   Christina Rossetti (1830–1894),"
    1930.B5

Hunt, Violet,    1932.B1

Hunt, William Holman,    1905.B1

"I Am Christina Rossetti,"
    1930.B12
    1932.B9

Impressions and Memories,    1895.B27

Ironside, Robin,    1953.B1

I Rossetti:  Storia di una Famiglia,    1928.B3

Japp, Alexander H.,    1895.B21

Jarvis, Kathleen,    1955.B3

Jennings, Elizabeth,    1970.B1

Johnson, Lionel,    1896.B13

Johnson, M.,    1895.B22

Jones, Howard Mumford,    1956.B3

Juhnke, Anna Kreider,    1966.A1

Kent, Muriel,    1930.B7

Kenyon, James Benjamin
    1896.B14
    1901.B2

Klenk, Hans,   1932.B2

Kohl, James A.,
    1968.B5
    1969.A3
    1971.B2

Lang, Andrew,   1895.B23

Last Sheaf: Essays,   1928.B4

Law, Alice,   1895.B24

Lawson, Malcolm,   1917.B1

Leaders of the Victorian Revolution,   1934.B1

Lead, Kindly Light: Studies of the Saints and Heroes of
    the Oxford Movement,   1932.B4

Le Gallienne, Richard,   1891.B2

Letter and Spirit,   1883.B2

Levy, Amy,   1888.B2

Lewis, Naomi,
    1959.B2
    1969.B1

Library of the World's Best Literature Ancient and Mod-
    ern,   1902.B1

"Life of Christina Rossetti" (Marshall),   1923.A1

Life of Christina Rossetti (Sandars),   1930.A3

Lingo, June Inez,   1930.A2

Literature of the Victorian Era,   1910.B4

Little Journeys to the Homes of Famous Women,   1897.B2

# Author/Title Index

Livingston, Luther S., 1899.B5

Loiterings in Old Fields: Literary Sketches, 1901.B2

"Love Affairs of Christina Rossetti," 1919.B3

Lowther, George, 1913.B2

Lubbock, Percy, 1918.B2

Lucas, F. L.,
    1940.B1
    1948.B1

Lynde, Richard D., 1965.B2

"Lyric Voice of Christina Rossetti," 1971.B1

Lyrics of Miss Rossetti, 1889.B2

McGill, Anna Blanche, 1900.B2

Mackenzie, Margaret, 1932.B3

Madeleva, M., 1925.B1

Maids of Honour, 1906.B2

Marshall, Dorothy Vesta, 1929.A1

Marshall, Louisville, 1923.A1

Martin, Helen Virginia, 1915.A1

Mason, Eugene, 1915.B1

Mather, Frank Jewett, Jr., 1919.B1

Maude, 1896.B4

# CHRISTINA ROSSETTI: A REFERENCE GUIDE

"Medical Comment on Christina Rossetti," 1968.B5

"Memoir," 1904.B10

Memorial Sermon Preached at Christ Church, Woburn Square,
for the Late Christina Georgina Rossetti, 1895.A1

Memories and Impressions: A Study in Atmospheres,
1911.B5

Men of the Time: A Dictionary of Contemporaries, Containing Biographical Notices of Eminent Characters
of Both Sexes, 1879.B1

Meynell, Alice,
1895.B25, B26
1910.B2
1947.B2

"Midsummer Eves of Shakespeare and Christina Rossetti,"
1972.B5

Midsummer Holiday and Other Poems, 1884.B1

Modern British Poetry: A Critical Anthology, 1936.B3.

Modern English Biography, 1901.B1

Moore, Virginia,
1930.B8
1934.B3

More Essays on Religion,
1927.B1
1928.B2

More, Paul Elmer,
1904.B8
1905.B2

Morse, B. J., 1931.B4

# Author/Title Index

Morse-Boycott, Desmond, 1932.B4

Murciaux, C. 1964.B1

"Music to Song of Christina Rossetti," 1917.B1, B3

Mystical Poets of the English Church, 1919.B2

Mysticism in the Neo-Romantics, 1923.B2

Nachwirkungen Dante Gabriel Rossettis, 1932.B2

Nash, Joseph John Glendinning,
    1895.B1
    1896.B15, B16

New Poems, 1896.B1, B2, B3, B5, B7, B8, B9, B17, B18, B21

"New Year's Eve: Christina Rossetti Died December 29,
    1894,"
    1895.B33
    1904.B12

Nicoll, W. Robertson [Claudius Clear], 1898.B8, B9

Noble, James Ashcroft
    1891.B3
    1895.B27

Norton, Mrs. Charles Eliot, 1863.B1, B2

"Not All Roses in the Victorian Nursery," 1951.B1

Notebooks and Papers of Gerard Manley Hopkins, 1937.B1

"Note on the Imagery in Christina Rossetti's 'A Birth-
    day,'" 1965.B2

Nuovi Saggi di Letteratura Inglese, 1918.B3

Obertello, Alfredo, 1931.B5

Obituary notices,
    1895.B1, B2, B3, B4, B5, B6, B7, B8, B9, B11, B12,
        B13, B31, B32, B33, B36, B37
    1896.B15, B16
    1898.B2
    1899.B1, B2

O'Brien, Mrs. William, 1912.B3

Old Familiar Faces, 1916.B1

Olivero, Federico, 1918.B3

Osmond, Percy H., 1919.B2

Our Living Poets: An Essay in Criticism, 1871.B2

Outlines of Victorian Literature, 1919.B4

Owen, Marion, 1970.B2

"'O Where Are You Going': W. H. Auden and Christina
    Rossetti," 1960.B1

"Oxford Movement and Its Influence on English Poetry,"
    1931.B7

Packer, Lona Mosk,
    1957.A1
    1958.B1
    1959.B3, B4
    1962.B2
    1963.A1, B2, B3
    1969.B2

Pageant and Other Poems,
    1881.B1, B2, B3, B4, B5, B6
    1882.B1
    1883.B1
    1887.B1
    1969.A4

"Panels in the Reredos in Christ Church, Woburn Square,
    London, In Memorial of Christina Rossetti," 1899.B2

Papers Critical and Reminiscent, 1912.B4

Parker, Elizabeth, 1919.B3

Payne, W. M.,
    1896.B17
    1902.B1

Personal Sketches of Recent Authors, 1898.B7

Peterson, Houston, 1929.B2

Poems (1890),
    1890.B1
    1891.B2
    1893.B3

Poems by Christina Rossetti (Ironside), 1953.B1

Poems by Christina Rossetti (Meynell), 1910.B2

Poems of Christina Rossetti (Golden Treasury Series),
    1904.B11

Poems of Christina Rossetti (Jarvis), 1955.B3

Poems of William Watson, 1905.B4

Poetical Works of Christina Georgina Rossetti (W. M.
    Rossetti), 1904.B10

Poetry and Prose of Christina Rossetti (Shalkhauser),
    1955.A2

"Poetry of Christina Rossetti" (Marshall), 1929.A1

Poets and the Poetry of the Nineteenth Century, 1907.B2

Poor Splendid Wings: The Rossettis and Their Circle,
    1934.B4

Porter, C.  1896.B18

Pre-Raphaelite Aesthetic and the Poetry of Christina
  Rossetti, William Morris, and William Butler Yeats,
  1967.B1

Pre-Raphaelite Poets (Stevenson),  1972.B7

Pre-Raphaelites (Buckley),  1968.B2

Pre-Raphaelitism: A Biblio-Critical Study,  1963.B1

Pre-Raphaelitism and the Pre-Raphaelite Brotherhood,
  1905.B1

Prince's Progress and Other Poems,
  1866.B1, B2, B3, B4, B5, B6, B7, B8, B9
  1867.B1
  1903.B2

Proctor, Ellen A.  1895.B2

Prose and Poetry (Meynell),  1947.B2

"Protestant Existentialism of Christina Rossetti,"
  1959.B4

Raleigh, Walter,
  1904.B9
  1938.B1

Reid, Stuart J.,  1905.B3

Reilly, Joseph J.,
  1931.B6
  1932.B5

Relativity and Polarity in Christina Rossetti,  1968.A1

Religious Trends in English Poetry, Volume IV, 1830-1880:
  Christianity and Romanticism in the Victorian Era,
  1957.B1

# Author/Title Index

Reticence in Literature, and Other Papers,   1915.B2

Ricks, Christopher,   1960.B1

Robb, Nesca Adeline,   1948.B2

Robertson, Eric S.,   1883.B1

Romantic Imagination,
    1949.B2
    1961.B1

Rossetti and His Circle,   1922.B1

Rossetti, Dante Gabriel,   1895.B28

Rossetti Family, 1824-1854,   1932.B8

Rossetti, Geoffrey W.,   1930.B9

Rossetti-Macmillan Letters:  Some 133 Unpublished Letters
    Written to Alexander Macmillan, F. S. Ellis, and
    Others, by Dante Gabriel, Christina, and William
    Michael Rossetti, 1861-1889,   1963.B2

Rossetti Papers, 1862 to 1870,   1903.B2

Rossettis:  Dante Gabriel and Christina,   1900.B1

Rossetti, William Michael
    1895.B29
    1903.B2
    1904.B10, B11
    1906.B5

Rudd, F. A.,   1867.B1

Rutherford, Mildred,   1906.B6

"Saint by Chance,"   1936.B2

Saintsbury, George
    1907.B1
    1910.B3

Sandars, Mary F., 1930.A3

"Santa Christina," 1912.B5, B6

Sawtell, Margaret, 1955.A1

Schappes, Morris U., 1932.B6

Seaman, Owen, 1896.B19

Second Common Reader, 1932.B9

Selected Poems of Christina G. Rossetti (Burke), 1913.B1

Selected Poems of Christina Rossetti (Zaturenska),
    1970.B3

Serra, Beatrice, 1929.B3

Shalkhauser, Marian Doris,
    1955.A2
    1956.B4

Sharp, William
    1886.B2, B3, B4
    1895.B30
    1912.B4

Shelburne Essays: Third Series, 1905.B2

Shipton, Irene A. M., 1933.B5

Short History of English Literature, 1907.B1

Short History of English Literature in the Nineteenth
    Century, 1918.B1

Shove, Fredegond, 1931.A1

Shuster, George N., 1922.B2

Simcox, G. A.,
    1870.B3
    1881.B7

Simcox, G. S., 1883.B2

Sing-Song, 1872.B1, B2, B3, B4

Sitwell, Edith    1942.B3

Smellie, A., 1895.B31

Smith, Ethel May, 1934.A1

Snow, Florence L., 1897.B3

"Some Notes on Christina Rossetti and Italy," 1931.B4

"Some Reminiscences of Christina Rossetti," 1895.B19,
    B20

Some Reminiscences of William Michael Rossetti, 1906.B5

Sonnets of Christina Rossetti:  A Comparative Prosodic
    Analysis, 1971.A1

"Sources of Christina Rossetti's 'Goblin Market,'"
    1933.B2

Sparks of Fire:  Christina Rossetti's Artistic Life,
    1969.A3

Speaking Likenesses
    1874.B1, B2
    1959.B1, B3

Sprachform der Lyrik Christina Rossettis, 1933.A2

Stedman, Edmund Clarence, 1887.B3

# CHRISTINA ROSSETTI: A REFERENCE GUIDE

Stevenson, Lionel, 1972.B7

Stewart, Bella Craig, 1933.A3

Storia della Letturatura Inglese, 1933.B1

Stuart, Dorothy Margaret,
   1930.A4
   1931.A2

Studies in Christina Rossetti's 'GOBLIN MARKET' AND OTHER
   POEMS, 1969.A1

Studies in Two Literatures,
   1897.B4
   1924.B1

"Study of the Poetry of Christina Rossetti" (Lingo),
   1930.A2

Survey of English Literature, 1780-1880: In Four Volumes, 1920.B1

Sutherland, D., 1895.B32

Swann, Thomas Burnett, 1960.A1

Swinburne, Algernon Charles
   1883.B3
   1884.B1
   1895.B33
   1904.B12

"Swinburne and Christina Rossetti: Atheist and
   Anglican," 1963.B3

"Symbol and Reality in Christina Rossetti's Goblin Market," 1958.B1

Symons, Arthur,
   1897.B4
   1907.B2
   1923.B3
   1924.B1

# Author/Title Index

Taylor, Bayard,
    1877.B1
    1880.B1

Teasdale, Sara, 1932.A1

Ten Victorian Poets, 1940.B1

Ten Victorian Poets (3rd ed.), 1948.B1

Thirlmere, Rowland, See Walker, John

Thomas, Edward, 1928.B4

Thomas, Eleanor Walter, 1931.A3

Thompson, A. Hamilton
    1901.B3
    1917.B2
    1933.B6

Three Rossettis: Unpublished Letters to and from Dante
    Gabriel, Christina, William, 1937.B2

Time Flies, 1886.B1

Troxell, Janet Camp, 1937.B2

Tuell, Anne Kimball, 1932.B7

"Two Christian Poets: Christina G. Rossetti and Paul
    Verlaine," 1915.B1

Tynan, Katharine, See Hinkson, Katharine Tynan

Uffelman, Larry Kent, 1969.A4

Unseen Friends, 1912.B3

Untermeyer, Louis, 1936.B3

"'Up-Hill' and 'Down'- by Christina Rossetti," 1972.B1

CHRISTINA ROSSETTI: A REFERENCE GUIDE

Venkatesan, N. K.,
    1913.B3
    1914.B1, B2

Verses (1893)
    1893.B4
    1894.B1

Vers la Joie,  1906.B3

Victorian at Bay,  1932.B7

Victorian Poetry (Brown),  1942.B2

Victorian Poets (Stedman),  1887.B3

Victorian Poets: A Guide to Research (Faverty),  1956.B3

Victorian Poets: A Guide to Research (2nd ed.),  1968.B3

Victorian Songs: Lyrics of the Affections and Nature,
    1895.B17

"Vita Aeterna: In Memoriam Christinae G. Rossetti,"
    1896.B20

"Voice from the World. Fragments of 'An Answer to Miss
    Rossetti's Convent Threshold,'"  1937.B1

Wainewright, John B.,  1917.B3

Walker, Hugh,
    1900.B3
    1910.B4
    1919.B4

Walker, John
    1889.B1, B2
    1896.B20

Walker, Mrs. Hugh,  1919.B4

# Author/Title Index

Waller, John O.,  1969.B3

Waller, R. D.,  1932.B8

Walters, Hildred A.,  1931.A4

Watson, Lily,
    1894.B2
    1895.B34

Watson, William,
    1905.B4
    1922.B3

Watts-Dunton, Theodore
    1895.B35, B36, B37
    1896.B21
    1906.B7
    1916.B1

Waugh, Arthur
    1915.B2
    1930.B10

Weathers, Winston,  1965.B3

Weideman, Rebecca S.,  1970.A1.  See also Crump, R. W.

Westcott, Brooke Foss,  1899.A1

Whitney, Elizabeth Boyce,  1931.B7

Wife of Rossetti:  Her Life and Death,  1932.B1

Wilkinson, David Carl,  1968.A2

Williamson, Claude C. H.,  1915.B3

Winwar, Frances, See Grebanier, Frances

Women-Writers of the Nineteenth Century,  1923.B1

Wonder and Whimsey:  The Fantastic World of Christina
    Rossetti,  1960.A1

Woods, Margaret L.,  1930.B11

Woolf, Virginia
    1930.B12
    1932.B9
    1953.B2

Writer's Diary:  Being Extracts from the Diary of
    Virginia Woolf,  1953.B2

Writers of Three Centuries:  1789-1914,  1915.B3

Wyzema, T. de,  1908.B2

Zabel, Morton D.,  1930.B13

Zaturenska, Marya,
    1949.A1
    1970.B3